A LIFE IN EXILE
Ugo Foscolo in London, 1816–1827

A LIFE IN EXILE
Ugo Foscolo in London, 1816–1827

Carlo Maria Franzero

W. H. ALLEN · LONDON
A Howard & Wyndham Company
1977

First published in Italian as *Ugo Foscolo a Londra*
First British edition © copyright by Carlo Maria Franzero, 1977

This book or parts thereof may not be
reproduced without permission in writing.

Printed and bound in Great Britain
by W & J Mackay Limited, Chatham
for the Publishers, W. H. Allen & Co. Ltd,
44 Hill Street, London W1X 8LB

ISBN 0 491 02281 6

*'Tieni per certo, donna mia, che
in questa terra troverò presto o
il cataletto o il carro trionfale.'*

Ugo Foscolo to the Donna Gentile,
25th October 1816

Contents

	Page
A Preface: Poetry and Exile by Roberto Ducci	ix
The Triumphal Chariot	1
Callirrhoe	39
The 'Digamma' Enterprise	67
The Catafalque	105

A Preface

POETRY AND EXILE

Are there people left in our times who still read *Parallel Lives* written by the Greek scholar Plutarch at the end of the first century AD, a book whose study was imposed ever since the Renaissance on generations and generations of pupils? Alexander and Caesar, Alcibiades and Coriolanus, Demosthenes and Cicero; generals, orators, statesmen and legislators were paired, compared, contrasted and conciliated. This superb gallery of twin heroes survived nearly two millennia, to the despair of students and the fascination of young people in pursuit of glory, greatest among them Napoleon.

In present times Plutarch and his *Parallel Lives* have ceased to torture or to inflame our sons. Asymmetry, not symmetry, is the fashion; Euclidean geometry is only one of the possible geometries; a catalogue of heroes would now include mostly football players, film stars and rock singers. The wind of change is recognizable and recognized; there are instances, however, when historians and readers might be tempted to regret the decline and disappearance of the Plutarchian methodology. This is the case when dealing with the protagonist of this biography, or perhaps semibiography, written by Carlo Maria Franzero (of whom later): Ugo Foscolo, the great Italian poet of the beginning of the Romantic era, whose life, character, works, passions, temperament, tastes and, in a word, destiny are remarkably similar to those of another poet at the inception of the Romantic revolution: George Gordon, Lord Byron, Foscolo's English twin.

My task as prefacer being that of introducing to the average reader of this book the Italian twin, whose name still adorns the literary Pantheon of his country but is now very little known in Britain, I shall attempt to fulfil it by putting him in parallel to his English double. Foscolo and Byron were contemporaries, having been born in 1778 and in 1788 respectively, and having died in 1827 and 1824. They were both noblemen, but Foscolo of less shining ancestry; both passionate and sometimes emotionally unstable; both carried away by the magic of poetry (though Foscolo wrote only one hundredth of the myriads of lines that Byron produced); both profligate in the use of money, the English lord having always plenty of it, the Venetian *nobiluomo* always too little. They attracted women of all sorts (and in Byron's case also a few boys) as easily as flowers attract butterflies; they convinced themselves every year that they were madly in love with a new person: and probably never loved any one of them, viewing their women as pleasurable landscapes which revealed themselves if illuminated by their ir-repressible lust for life and then vanished again into the night. Both were non-conformists and flirted with Jacobins; and were afflicted by a contradiction frequent in their times, as indeed was Beethoven: they fought for freedom and at the same time admired Buonaparte (if not Napoleon).

Celebrity kissed both Foscolo and Byron at the age of 24: 'they woke up one morning and found themselves famous', Foscolo in 1802 for a novel resonant with Wertherian echoes, *The Last Letters of Jacopo Ortis*, Byron in 1812 for *Childe Harold*. They both enter-tained an intermittent correspondence with the Great Old Man of European poetry, Wolfgang von Goethe. Like his, their literary formation had been rooted in the classics, and their inspiration came frequently (more so in Foscolo than in Byron) from the Greco-Roman heritage; but, like Goethe in Germany, they opened the gates in Italy and Britain to the onward-marching Romantic army, which during the next century and a half occupied and firmly held in the whole of Western Europe not only the realm of the arts, but the kingdoms of politics, taste and social habits; appealing, not with-out disastrous effects, to passion against reason and to *hubris* against balance. Foscolo and Byron were considered in Italy and in Great Britain respectively the greatest poets of their era, which they were not. The really great Italian poet of the period was Leopardi, the English one was Keats (at least in my judgment). But in the twins' breasts blew the Promethean spirit which often moves men to great things, even if seldom to great poems. Both men were ruled by an internal *daimon*, which at least in Byron's case was a close relative of the Devil.

Foscolo and Byron never met and probably knew little or nothing of each other's works, though Byron's knowledge of Italian was better than Foscolo's of English. Parallel as their destinies were, their steps never crossed. They were never in England at the same time, but frequented at different times the same great houses, for instance Holland House; they had the same publisher, John Murray II; they were both friends of John Cam Hobhouse. They were never at the same time in Venice or in Italy, though Contessa Guiccioli had more than one point in common with Contessa Albrizzi. They were relatively close in space only in 1816, most of which they spent in Switzerland; but Byron was staying in Geneva and Berne before proceeding to his self-imposed exile in Italy, and Foscolo in Zurich and Basle as a fugitive from the Austrian domination restored in Lombardy and Venetia. They were each born close to the place where the other was going to die. The ship which in 1823 took Byron to the Greek mainland, where he would perish the following year, scudded past the Ionian island of Zante or Zacynthus—the Hyacinth isle—where Foscolo had been born 45 years earlier. Four years later Foscolo died in London, not far from one of the Devonshire residences where Byron had danced with Lady Caroline Lamb in 1812, the year of their love and hate, the newly imported waltz.

The analogy between the two poets should not be pushed too far. They shared, perhaps not always consciously, the rather confused identification of life and art—personal life as a work of art, art as the uncontrolled expression of one's predestined character—which was the vaporous essence of the *Weltanschauung* of Romanticism. But circumstances of life often defile and obfuscate artistic consciousness. It so happened to Foscolo, who in 1816 arrived in London with the halo of a freedom fighter (a protagonist of dissent, we could call him now) and of a great poet. A few years later his whole patrimony of good-will and his own means of subsistence had been dissipated: he had been, in John Donne's words, his 'own executioner'. He had enjoyed the miracle of the affection of a newly found natural daughter, Floriana, born to a young Englishwoman, Fanny Emerytt, with whom he had had a fugitive love affair at Valenciennes in 1804, while Napoleon's Grande Armée, in which he was then serving, was expecting the signal for the invasion of Britain. But Poetry was dead in his bosom, and he himself died in loneliness, misery and illness at the age of 49. His grave in the cemetery at Chiswick was paid for by the few friends, mostly Italians, whom he had not lost; and his bones were to remain there, slowly forgotten by everybody, until they were transferred in 1871 to the glory of Santa Croce in Florence.

Exile seems often to be the natural crowning of a poet's life. So it is in particular during certain historical periods, but more especially in the case of English and Italian poets. Though they were prompted to abandon their native countries by political or mundane oppression, there is a subtler affinity between exile and poetry. It was actually one of the tenets of the creed of Romanticism that a poet was by nature an exile on earth, having forsaken the realm which is his own and which may be approximately situated beyond the rainbow. But even in times like ours which are not romantic (without yet being classical), exile is growing into a recognized institution. We all know of Russian poets who, like Pasternak, died as exiles in their own country, and of others who, like Solzhenitsin, have been forced to wander in foreign lands. It is an age-old story: they may find comfort in comparing themselves to Ovid or Dante who were also ostracized; but it will be a scant comfort, because their souls too will be surrounded by *tristia* and their lips will taste the bitterness of the bread given by an alien hand.

The sad story of the last twelve years of Foscolo's life in London as a political exile is recounted in this book by Carlo Maria Franzero with the same historical accuracy and the same literary verve which have made some of his other books, such as *The House of Mrs Caroline*, *Nero* or *Cleopatra*, world bestsellers. But the tale is unfolded with greater affection for the protagonist. Franzero came to Britain as a journalist in 1922, and has settled here since, not leaving the land of his choice even during the Second World War. His own exile, unlike that of Foscolo, has been successful; he has found in this country fame and tranquillity, as well as friends and women to enliven his younger and his older years. He is as English as an Italian can be who has lived in Great Britain for 55 years; he writes his books in English, but continues to contribute to Italian newspapers. Franzero seems to the author of this preface (*pro-tempore* Italian Ambassador to the Court of St James's, and an old friend of the British people) a perfect example of the symbiosis between Italians and Britishers, upon which some of the hopes for a more stable Union of Europe can be founded.

But a tenuous feeling of nostalgia can sometimes pierce the conscience even of a man who has lived so long abroad. When the sun sets beyond the trees that mark the horizon of the Surrey countryside where Franzero's Regency house is situated; when the birds are muted by the twilight, and the colours of the flowers change to pale grey, and the lawn is a carpet for the whippet to lie on: in that deep silence Franzero's ears (which are still very good, as are his eyes, notwithstanding his advanced age) catch the distant, oh how distant, sounds of his youth in Turin. The splendid and chilly sovereign city of Piedmont, whence Cavour conducted the unification of Italy with the aim of establishing an English-style constitutional system, emerges from the depths of the past in full armour, her spires, steeples, and towers looming against the snow-white Alps. For a brief moment, before he awakens to his normal condition of country squire and English author, Franzero feels again in his heart what it is to be a refugee. It is thanks to this fleeting sensation that he has been able to describe with sympathy and understanding the last years of the life of Ugo Foscolo, poet and political exile, who died in London one hundred and fifty years ago.

ROBERTO DUCCI
April 1977

Roberto Ducci, born several years ago into a Florentine family, is a professional diplomat, and has represented Italy at the Court of St James's since 1975. He is also a writer, historian and journalist; and has published five books and numerous articles, being a regular contributor to the great Milan newspaper *Corriere della Sera.*

The Triumphal Chariot

I

Foscolo arrived in London on 11th September 1816, to begin in earnest his life in exile. He was thirty-eight years old.

His exile had, in fact, commenced the previous year with his flight into Switzerland, when life among the ruins of the Italian Kingdom had become impossible, not to say dangerous for him. Several of his friends had already been arrested by the Austrians. His own offer to create a newspaper or a periodical had been turned by Marshal Bellegarde into a proposal to place his pen at the service of the government, which was not exactly in the interests of Italy, and Foscolo could not forget what he had written, in November 1813, to the Viceroy Eugène de Beauharnais: 'The sorrows of my country may sadden me, but they will never induce me to serve the cause of any other prince.' It was a solemn engagement that he had taken with himself. And now, to break entirely with Austria was tantamount to giving up that pension which he considered he had earned by his military service, and which was his only source of livelihood. By February 1815 his negotiations for a newspaper had progressed sufficiently for him to prepare a scheme for a paper to be submitted to the government for approval.

'Every reigning house,' he had written, 'needs, and has the right and the duty to bring public opinion into the system of government; and the means of achieving this must be delicate indeed.' Yet those words had burned his fingers.

All things considered, the best solution was for him to await a suitable moment to act: to run away from Italy, run away from Milan, and go into exile. He kept that decision strictly to himself, to avoid the government becoming suspicious and prevent him from doing it. At last, on 30th March, without a passport and without money, he ran away to Switzerland. The following day he wrote the well-known letter to his family:

'My honour and conscience prevent me from giving the guarantee that the present government expects from me forcing me to

3

serve in the militia. . . . Besides, I should betray that nobleness of character, intact until now, of swearing to do a thing which I could not do, and selling myself, in this way, to any government. . . . If, therefore, dear mother, I go into exile and place myself as a refugee in the hands of Fortune and of Heaven, you will surely not blame me, as you yourself inspired and implanted with your milk these honourable sentiments, and have often urged me to respect them.'

But although the flight was successfully accomplished, exile in Switzerland was very bitter. And later on, he could not help remembering the occasion when one of the pack animals fell and his few possessions were scattered, breaking the bottles of oils and essences that diffused their fragrance into the air. He got so cross at the loss of his toilet articles that he lost his temper, to the stupefaction of his friend Professor Catenazzi, who was escorting him.

His intention on leaving Italy was to go at once to England, as his friend Stewart Rose had advised him to do; but as it had not been possible to obtain passports via Antwerp, and thinking it wiser to avoid France, there was no other way but to remain for a while in Switzerland.

From Como he had walked as far as Lugano, where he found hospitality with the printer Francesco Veladini, who was the publisher of the *Gazzetta di Lugano*; but a few days later, the Ticino Government being too subservient to Austria, he had taken to the road again, and crossing Mount Ceneri had gone to Roveredo in the Grisons. But not even in Roveredo was the atmosphere favourable; he was now watched and followed; in Milan the Strassoldo was storming the representative of the Swiss Confederation and the magistracy of various cantons with requests 'not to give peace to the notorious ex-militiaman Ugo Foscolo'. At the beginning of May he had again taken to the road, and after a short rest in Cubbiolo, another at Coira and one more at Saint Gall, arrived in Zurich on 23rd May.

This wearisome travelling had consumed most of his small supply of money, and he certainly would not have enough to start for England. On 2nd June he wrote to his friend Trechi in Milan, telling him that he barely had enough to carry on for three months.

His only good fortune was that Count Capodistria made enquiries about him through the Russian Legation, and this ensured him safe shelter among the Swiss. And when he found a little peace, he worked on the preparation of the *Ipercalisse*, and also took up the translation of Homer, writing and rewriting six lines a day. Yet, would he ever forget the terrible days he had spent in the house of the Protestant Vicar of Hottingen, who gave him nothing to eat but boiled meat and some terrible soups that were ruining his stomach? In the vicar's house the bread was bought in town each Monday, and given to him for the rest of the week. His belongings were pilfered, his fine linen shirts changed for common ones of coarse cotton. At the beginning of October, after paying a quarter's rent in advance and purchasing some tea, paper, ink, sugar and candles, all he had left was a solitary little silver coin worth fifteen pence.

On 31st October a letter arrived from Quirina Magiotti. It was Saint Quirino's day, and so strongly was he struck by the coincidence, almost a divine event, that he could not restrain his tears. Ah, why had he so cruelly forgotten his *Donna Gentile*? Quirina was writing 'almost with a shaking hand on 19th June, just recovering from a serious illness', and she was reproaching him for not having given news of himself since January, though she had written to him time after time, offering everything that was in her power to give him. Now she was repeating her offers.

Yes, Quirina, the good and devoted *Donna Gentile*, was offering, as she had always done, anything that was in her power to give. There was still somebody who lived for him, who was thinking of him, and would not let him die; warm-hearted Quirina whom he had treated so badly, with such cruel indifference, in Florence and Milan. Now he regretted not having thought of her; and indeed looked among his papers for a letter which he had begun in Milan in March before his flight. He added only one page:

> 'I will not lie; my affairs are really very bad, although I am not in need, and to prevent you from worrying about me I will add that I do not possess much, but I need very little.'

He had felt ashamed of telling her the whole truth, because he was already in debt to Quirina who, though he did not know it, had always burned all his promissory notes. To tell her 'all the truth' would have been tantamount to asking her for more money, and yet he was in such dire poverty that a few days later he wrote to his friend Trechi begging a small loan: 'I am ready for anything, and seeing how people are abandoning me helps me to strengthen my soul against death.'

On 10th December he felt reduced to sending Quirina a promissory note for 58 Florentine lire, for fifteen days. While waiting to hear from Trechi and Quirina, being unable to pay his next quarter's rent, he went around the town trying to sell his watch and fob and two small gold rings. The jewellers looked suspiciously at this foreigner with his soft hands and shabby clothes trying to sell such a fine gold repeater.

Trechi, who was already owed 400 lire, sent another 150 and Quirina sent the 58 Florentine lire, apologizing for not having sent more before, and telling him that she was prepared to send him a regular sum every three months. What Foscolo did not know was that Quirina had begged the Countess of Albany to lend her the lovely portrait of Ugo painted by Fabre, and that she had had a copy made of it and had put it in her bedroom covered with a veil. At night, before going to bed, she would lift the veil and devotedly kiss the dear features of her beloved Ugo.

In December Count Capodistria, passing through Switzerland, went to visit him, showing him great courtesy and making him several offers of help, and treating him with such cordiality that his Swiss landlord thought Foscolo must be a man of high rank. Count Capodistria volunteered to intercede for Foscolo in Vienna; but Foscolo begged him to do nothing, and was satisfied by Capodistria's promise to make sure that his mother's affairs in Zante would be safeguarded.

And now there remained only the decision to go to England. He wrote about it to Quirina, who nearly fainted when she read his letter: 'I am worried,' she replied, 'I am truly worried at your plan to go to England, for deep in my heart I have an uneasy feeling that I shall never see you again.' (And how right she was!) And in March 1816 Quirina wrote to Ugo that she now possessed his portrait: 'I look at you and I feel that I am seeing my Ugo of long ago, on the day that I met you between the Ponte Vecchio and the New Market, and my heart fluttered so violently! Yet I had never spoken to you, but my heart spoke before my mouth, with the same emotion that at this very moment makes me unable to hold my pen. . . . But now I have your portrait before me, and the resemblance could not be more perfect; and (how can I tell you?) I do not dare to touch your face with my lips, for there is more soul than body in this portrait, and I am almost afraid to profane it. . . .'

During the month of March, in Zurich, he had a romantic affair with Veronica Pestalozzi, the wife of the Italian banker Solomon Pestalozzi: could Foscolo's life ever proceed without a small romance? But it was a sad love affair—indeed an ugly one, for which he afterwards felt ashamed. The banker Pestalozzi, whom Foscolo had met in Milan when he was working in Porta's Bank—and it had been Gaspare Porta who had given him a letter for Pestalozzi's wife—had invited Foscolo to his house to introduce him to her. To tell the truth, Madame Pestalozzi had not appeared very attractive to Foscolo who loved soft curves in women, while Veronica was rather bony and far from beautiful, her mouth spoiled by scurvy which at that time had affected many Swiss women. Yet her lips were vividly red, and amid so much desolation Foscolo found her a lady of some elegance: 'tall, very slender, with beautiful black eyes, and Italian fair hair, and full of life and conversation, and always elegantly dressed. . . .' This is how Ugo described her in a letter to Quirina when he later told her about the strange misadventure.

After a few weeks of acquaintance—he was visiting her each Wednesday—Foscolo told Veronica that he loved her; and Veronica answered: 'I have, alas, noticed it, and I feel sorry for you. . . .' The reason was that Madame Pestalozzi already had a lover, a certain Guido Sorelli who was giving her Italian lessons. But Ugo persisted with his protestations, that were a repetition of all the love affairs he had had with so many other women. But one day Veronica sent him the letters from all her other lovers, with a copy of a letter she had written to one of them *'pour vous aider à me connaître entièrement'*. It was the foolish gesture of a hysterical woman, which indeed Veronica was, and some days later Foscolo did a quite incredible thing. He disclosed to Solomon Pestalozzi the love affair between his wife and Sorelli. Afterwards Foscolo called this 'his crime'.

During those same months he met Matilde Viscontini Dembrowski again, a sweet, courageous woman who, in an effort to escape her brutal husband, was dragging her unhappy marriage through Switzerland—from Berne to Vevey. Foscolo was always becoming involved with women.

Yet in that very month of March he had written to Quirina: 'Although I am so anxious to get away from this fatal country, I would not like to go too far away.' And in the same letter he had offered to marry Quirina: 'Mother to me, and bride and sister and mistress. . . . Oh, Quirina, a sister in the tempest.' But Quirina had nobly and wisely declined: 'You would lose the only precious gift you still possess, your freedom and absolute independence; I could not give you what I do not possess: the beauty which nature has denied me. When you come back we shall be two inseparable friends till death parts us, and if it is my good fortune to devote my life and all my attention to you, and to live with you under the same roof, and not to talk ever again of what is mine and what is yours, all that is mine shall be yours too, and this will be my happiness.'

Yet it was Quirina who provided him with the means to leave for London, though he did not know it. Foscolo had asked Silvio Pellico in Milan to endeavour to sell such of his books as had remained there and on 20th April he wrote rather proudly to Quirina: 'I do not need any more money, as Silvio has been able to sell for 120 gold zecchini all the books I had left in Milan.' Quirina never let him know that the sale of his books had been her generous fiction, to enable her to send to him the money without revealing the source. And she also sent him a secretary, the young Andrea Calbo, who had already worked for him as a copyist in Florence and Bellosguardo.

In that same period his brother Giulio managed to send Ugo another hundred louis: altogether a few thousand lire—not much, but it seemed a great deal to Foscolo, who wrote to Quirina asking how much he owed her. On 14th May Quirina replied: 'You have asked me for an account; here it is with my full receipt. Do not ever mention the question of money; when Fortune enables you to return to Tuscany then we will talk of it, if at all. For the moment leave me the joy of being able now and then to offer you my helping hand, I beg you most sincerely.' Exquisite Quirina, so good and generous, who was able to see things as they really were and might for ever be!

By the end of July the new edition of the *Jacopo Ortis* which he had had privately printed by the Zurich publishers, Orell Fussli & Co. of Zurich, was ready, bearing the imprint: '*Ultime Lettere di Jacopo Ortis, Edizione XV ed unica fatta sopra la prima; Londra, MDCCCXIV*'. This was the private edition which he meant to take to London, and at the end of July Foscolo actually prepared to depart for England with Calbo. From that moment he began to feel serene and content, for now the idea of going to England floated in his mind like an invitation. What of the Italy of which he had written and spoken so much? The heavens were now compelling him to cast his die: and if it turned up for a country so glorious and rich as England, this would be a sign that fortune was on his side. He was ready to write to some friends in London to find for him 'a nice house', as he had done in Pavia when he had gone to take his Chair of Italian Literature that unfortunately vanished immediately after his inaugural lecture.

At last, on 7th September, a few minutes before taking ship from Ostend, he wrote to his mother: 'The wind is favourable, the sea is fine and the weather is calm. Tomorrow morning I shall be in England, and the day after tomorrow in London before midday.'

Wishes for a happy journey had been sent by Quirina through Calbo, in a letter inside which were a few blades of grass picked at Bellosguardo. And that day Quirina had told Calbo to close his eyes, and upon the lips of the young man she had placed a kiss for Ugo.

II

So Foscolo arrived in London on 11th September 1816 with his secretary and companion Andrea Calbo. To save expense he had travelled from Basle on the Rhine, then crossed the Channel from Ostend, but in such tempestuous weather that the journey took more than forty-three hours. Travelling expenses had considerably lightened Foscolo's purse; nevertheless, when at long last he arrived in London, he was still rich in hope and in good health. He took rooms at the Hotel Sablonnière in Leicester Square; but after a week transferred himself with Calbo to a suite of pleasant rooms at number 11 Soho Square.

During the first week of August Foscolo had spent a few days in Berne with an English traveller, Samuel Edward Cook, and had given the Englishman letters of introduction to Giuseppe Grassi and Quirina Magiotti in Florence, while Cook had given Foscolo a letter for Mr Sicard of the Princess of Wales's household at Kensington Palace, asking his friend to assist Foscolo to find suitable lodgings in London. Foscolo had also collected the addresses of a fair number of English people whom he had met in Italy, and lost no time in getting in touch with them. Sigismondo Trechi, who was in London, very promptly notified Foscolo's arrival to his friend Giuseppe Binda, who was working as a librarian in the house of the celebrated Lord Holland, whose house was the greatest political and literary salon in London. He at once expressed his desire to meet Foscolo, and a letter from Foscolo to Binda dated 17th September shows that Binda had already called upon him. Foscolo enclosed a note for Trechi, who received it on 22nd September and promptly answered it congratulating him upon his safe arrival. Trechi at that moment in Perth in Scotland in the '*amenissima villa*' of Mr Ferguson, wrote: 'I am sure that by this time you have met Lord Holland; what do you think of this most amiable and popular person? It is almost impossible to find a warmer heart; and I know that he thinks a lot of you.'

In the course of the first three days of his stay in London Foscolo

11

had also written to Sir Robert Wilson, whom he had met in Milan during 1814, and he also received from Canon Charles Parr-Burney, brother of the novelist Fanny Burney, a very kind invitation to visit him in Greenwich.

Truly, no sooner had he touched English soil than 'all things were pleasant, even the sun'. He poured out his happiness in a letter to Quirina: 'Were it not that the sun looks hazy in the early hours of sunrise, it would really give the lie to those who complain about the English fog.' Naturally, the happiest thing was for him to find himself 'received as a man of the highest reputation'. That letter to Quirina was a hymn of joy: 'My sweetest friend, holy as a mother to me and beloved like a sister, and dear as a wife and mistress—if there is in love a more venerated name, it is yours.' He told Quirina that he would soon be spending a couple of weeks with his friend Rose in the country, more than a hundred miles from London. In the meantime he had found 'a most decent house, quiet and gentlemanly, for twelve golden sovereigns per month'. That to him seemed a lot, but everybody told him it was a very modest rent. This letter, however, conveyed a sad thought: the fear that he would soon find himself very short of money. After reckoning with Calbo, Foscolo had come to the conclusion that to live in London would cost no less than £500 a year.

That he would soon be short of money he had felt from the very first days in London and he had written to his brother Giulio. But on 4th October his brother replied that he was utterly unable to send him 25 louis and could only send him 25 crowns.

On 25th October Foscolo wrote to the family: 'I beg forgiveness for the trouble I have given Giulio and all of you, and for the pain that my poverty has caused you. And to Giulio I say that I was obliged to worry him the very day I arrived in London, finding myself lost in such a multitude of people and heartless friends without a penny to buy a glass of water, because in this country even water costs a great deal.'

Words very different from those that he had written that same day to Quirina telling her that he had found it necessary to visit friends residing in the country, hundreds of miles away from London: 'Of this you may rest assured, beloved, that in this land I shall soon find either a bier or a triumphal chariot.'

He was not, therefore, as poor as he was indicating to his family; but the future was frightening.

It was easy to get drunk on illusion in London, because in 1816 the capital retained the exhilaration that had been born on 11th April 1814, soon after the fall of Napoleon, and had culminated in the victory of Waterloo on 18th June 1815. For nearly two years London had fêted the victors, and then peace had come, the panacea of all evils. The Allied Sovereigns had visited London escorted by their victorious generals, and the English armies had come back from the long war. For nearly two solid years there had been banquets, balls and entertainments in private houses and clubs. Every night before dinner there was the promenade in the park, where the crowd assembled to see the extravagantly dressed Regent, the ineffable and almost grotesque Prince Florizel, either on horseback or in a carriage. Then there were the ladies of fashion in their elegant coaches, with footmen in powdered wigs and vast cloaks that made them look like archbishops. The deer gambolled among the trees and brooks ran along green fields and woods. It was a lovely, almost romantic view. At night there was wild gambling; the gay, brightly uniformed officers courted the ladies with no less ardour than they had fought the war against Napoleon, and cheerfully lost their accumulated pay; and the eldest sons, who out of respect to posterity had not gone to war, were now duty bound to be generous to their younger brothers, and all these young men were crowding round the green tables in clubs whose members bore the finest names in the land.

Since the summer of 1815 a wealthy and secure England had been celebrating the peace, while Europe licked her wounds, and by 1816 London was still showing foreign visitors splendid and almost insolent opulence. The great houses were impressive with their ostentatious dinners and the richness of their decoration. In the capital and the surrounding countryside, the ancient houses were as splendid as royal palaces, while high society was living like a class that enjoyed inexhaustible wealth.

Moreover, after twelve years, the English could at long last cross the Channel once more and see Europe. Englishmen had always been the richest and most enthusiastic tourists. In addition to the excitement of setting foot again upon a soil for so many years denied them, was a reawakened curiosity and a desire to resume contact with the literature and ideas of the Continent. It was felt in London that while in England, under the necessities of the long years of war, social and political development had advanced under the impulse of incomparable individual energy, in France and in the other European countries, subjugated first by terror and then by a despotic militarism, civil progress had remained stagnant. And alongside the brilliant social life there had been developing in London intellectual groups anxious to make contact again with the talented Europeans who were beginning to arrive in England. The most brilliant meeting-place was Holland House, the stupendous residence of the Earls of Holland.

Holland House was almost a royal palace, a Court in which Lord and Lady Holland received anyone with a famous name or high reputation.

Foscolo, who had arrived in London with his fame as a poet and patriotic lover of liberty unsullied, was immediately fêted. Had he, in the past, fought in Napoleon's army? Yes, but that had been the army of freedom for the Italians. Besides, he had afterwards refused to become the Emperor's official poet and the Viceroy had denied him his protection. And after the Austrians returned to Milan, Foscolo was reduced to running away to escape the fate of many others, of imprisonment in the Spielberg.

Hence the warmth of his welcome. The poet Samuel Rogers, who was also a banker, immediately became his friend and offered his services. And Lord Holland and others were enchanted by the vivacity of the Italian poet, who was a good speaker and debater, with a fiery imagination and immense culture.

Foscolo was one of those rare men who are at once the centre of attraction wherever they are. A drawing-room became his lecture-room: he did not listen to other speakers, but made others listen to him. And English society did listen to him. He was surrounded by an aura of poetic glory, of political scandals and also of love; he was an Italian Byron. Even his way of dressing caught the eye, and his ugly face appeared fascinating. He spoke more French than English, and often made long speeches in Italian; but the society of Holland House was cultured, and everybody spoke French fluently, and many could read and understand Italian. Lord Holland said: 'We are all *engoués* with him'; and it was the highest compliment that could be paid.

Since the time when Byron had departed from England in bad humour and with a train of carriages and servants, no one in London had been more interesting than Foscolo.

As for Foscolo, Holland House had appeared to him a house beyond comparison with the houses he had visited in Milan or in Florence: it was grandiose, noble and elegant, without vulgarity or superficiality. Compared with Holland House, the palace of the Countess of Albany in Florence, notwithstanding the shadow of the Alfieri, was only a huge palace, into which anyone with some reputation could enter to gossip and speak maliciously about the world. The society one met in Holland House was entirely different. There one encountered a vast gathering of scientists and men of letters and culture, and as well as the aristocracy and foreign ambassadors there were men whose sole virtue was their intellect and their works, and all of them mixed with ease, and their conversation was always natural and varied.

Lady Holland reminded Foscolo a little of the Countess of Albany, already advancing in years, but still a good-looking woman. The Countess of Albany knew how to appear proud or affable, kind or malicious, elegant or slovenly, but Lady Holland needed none of these tricks.

Foscolo felt that he was in a new world: a world that wanted nothing better than to admit him as an equal.

Two years previously in Milan he had gone through a phase of extreme depression, and his only comfort had been the chance of making friends with William Stewart Rose, who was at that time visiting Italy; meeting again in England was a joy for both. Rose, who lived at Mudeford near Lyndhurst in Hants, sent his valet to London to guide Foscolo and gave him a letter of introduction to the Secretary of State who could help him to get over the rules that limited the movements of foreigners newly arrived in England. The visit to Mudeford, however, could not be made until the beginning of October, as Foscolo was suffering from a fever. Rose wrote urging him to move down to Mudeford where 'the sea air was regenerating', and mentioned that he could travel with Count Matexà, whom Foscolo already knew. Rose also enclosed a letter of introduction to Dr Martin Davy, Head of Caius College Oxford, mentioning *Madame son épouse* to whom Foscolo could teach some

Venetian songs to show that he was a well-tamed lion.

The journey was further delayed by Calbo's falling ill, but at last the visit to Mudeford took place, and gave much pleasure to both Foscolo and Rose. Upon his return to London Foscolo found a letter from Lord Holland inviting him again to Holland House to meet some friends who might be useful to him in his literary work, enclosing a letter of introduction for the publishers Longman and John Murray. Longman met Foscolo rather coolly, but Murray immediately gave him a contract for a series about the customs, letters and the political history of Italy, to be published in three volumes.

The first month in London had, therefore, been from the social point of view a complete success, with invitations arriving from everywhere and the nobility anxious to meet 'the famous Italian poet' and introduce him to anyone who could be useful to him. Foscolo repaid this hospitality and courtesy with fine letters and copies of his works, of which he had brought a good number to England.

But the voyage from Zurich had cost him £68 and he had arrived in London with barely enough to carry on even modestly till winter. The actual cost of travel to the houses where he was invited and the short trip to Lyndhurst had caused him some anxiety. Already on 19th September in a letter to his *Donna Gentile* he had mentioned his 'efforts to appear to new friends in good circumstances so as to succeed in maintaining a foothold'.

This problem—to appear in good circumstance—became for him a real obsession. It did not take him very long to realise that he must be sure to have £500 a year if he wanted to retain Calbo as his secretary, and the problem was how to earn £500 a year. Someone suggested that he give public lectures, that were quite fashionable between January and August. An excellent idea, but January was still far away, and his money was getting low. His appeal to his brother had failed; the family in Italy was poor, and they could not understand the needs of this son in London who found it necessary to lead a brilliant social life.

From Florence, however, Quirina, with her maternal instinct, at once realised the true state of things from Ugo's letters. On 23rd October Ugo acknowledged receipt of 30 zecchini ostensibly sent to Calbo, and almost reproached her for this very useful gesture, yet it gave him a chance to appreciate Quirina's kindness in understanding that the hospitality of the great world must be accepted in a grand manner, and he threw away the mask: 'Alas! I need other people's help, and to obtain it I must spend more than I can. But in this country it is a sin to be poor; no one would look at you . . .' Oh, the anguish of being reduced to put such a confession on paper! 'Even the price of the mail is becoming an expense to be met as rarely as possible', he wrote to Quirina, but he added that fortunately his health was good, though he blamed the fog for affecting his eyes and lungs. Now he was a prisoner of the fog, and endeavoured to pass the time in writing a long article against Chateaubriand's *Bonaparte et les Bourbons*, which however he did not succeed in getting published.

There was a much graver problem hanging over his head.

III

Prior to Foscolo's departure from Zurich the printers and publishers Orell, Fussli and Company had asked him to buy and send them from London a supply of English vellum for drawings. Foscolo had lost no time in attending to the matter, and was introduced to Angiolo Bonelli who was something between a middleman and a money-lender, and offered to do the deal for him. Foscolo handed Bonelli the money and was given a proper receipt. Bonelli explained to Foscolo that it would have been better and cheaper to buy the paper directly from the manufacturers, and this would have avoided customs charges. One Sunday evening in the middle of November Bonelli arrived at the poet's house telling him with great indignation that his own confidential secretary had disappeared with some two thousand pounds, and that consequently he, Bonelli, disclaimed any responsibility for the non-fulfilment of the paper deal for Zurich.

The loss of £42 was considerable, and Foscolo could not tolerate being cheated. He sued Bonelli, but an unfortunate fall and injury to his leg prevented him from being present in court; and as his friend Carlo Fillica explained that litigation in England was a costly game, he abandoned the lawsuit and to prevent the Zurich printers from suffering any damage, particularly in view of their letters of surprise and protest, Foscolo looked elsewhere for the paper, paying for it with a promissory note. But when the note was due he was very short of cash; and in March 1817, faced with the risk of going to prison, he looked wildly round for ways to get out of his difficulties.

This unpleasant adventure, so soon after his arrival in England, was typical of the rest of Foscolo's stay in London: a life that was always dark, where even the oases of pleasure were always overcast by clouds of sadness and misery.

One of his biographers, a contemporary and friend, was to write that if Foscolo had known how to balance his budget, he would have been able to live in London quite happily. This was an over-simplification, but a poet's life is a delicate web of pain and joy, of moral renunciation and material suffering.

19

Indeed, having learnt nothing from experience, Foscolo once again entrusted the commission of the paper to a sort of agent by the name of George Mills, who kindly accepted from Foscolo a bill for payment in three months. But at the due date, finding himself in even more dire circumstances, Foscolo was reduced to asking for a month's extension. By then, however, things had not improved, and confronted once again with the possibility of a debtors' prison, Foscolo addressed himself in desperation to General Sir Robert Wilson, begging him to save him from such a disgrace, and promising to repay him as soon as he could negotiate a loan of £200 against his houses in the Ionian Islands—'*autrement j'attendrai avec résignation tout ce qui pourra m'arriver, et j'aurai toujours dans mon âme le remords de vous avoir vainement affligé.*' The letter was rather absurd, and it is not clear whether the General was moved by the humiliating prayers of the poet; however, the letter of credit for £200 was discounted by banker Frederick Grig, whom Foscolo had fortunately met, and a substantial balance remained in the ever-needful hands of Foscolo.

Worst of all was the fact that neither the first nor the second shipment of the famous paper had taken place, and from Zurich the manager of Orell and Fussli, Monsieur Hagenbuch, protested vigorously. Foscolo had to break his silence and told Monsieur Hagenbuch the whole sad story in two long letters, one in February and the other on 4th March, with an explanation that sounded rather specious: '*Il me faut une protestation de votre part qui déclare que le papier, n'étant arrivé dans le temps promis faute de prompte expédition,' vous réclamez votre argent, et vous avez laissé la marchandise à la douane.*' The Zurich printers hastened to send the required declaration. We do not know what Foscolo did with that document, but at long last, one year afterwards, on 6th May 1818, Hagenbuch announced that the paper had arrived!

No sooner was the fracas over the paper behind Foscolo than another catastrophe occurred. In the month of February 1817, during which Foscolo had succeeded with much trouble in obtaining an extension of his promissory note to Mills for the Zurich paper (which was not sent), his litigation with Angelini began. Edmondo Angelini was an Italian from Friuli who, having emigrated to London, had devoted himself to teaching the Italian language, an occupation that was producing little money and even less reputation. Angelini printed a few booklets and addressed himself to Foscolo to recommend to him a good bookseller. As Foscolo took no notice Angelini revenged himself with the most vulgar insults. Violent letters were exchanged; then Angelini tried to seek a better fortune in Holland, Germany and France, till he finally returned to London poorer than before. There he changed his tune with Foscolo, despatching the most abject supplications: 'Covered with shame and with desperation in my heart, I beg and implore your help, having no bread nor courage to ask anyone else for it.' And forgetting his past abuse, he now called the poet 'the honourable Foscolo, who always enjoyed the reputation of being magnificent and generous'.

Foscolo did not take the bait, and limited himself to sending a small sum so as to preserve his reputation as a great poet and great gentleman. Angelini persisted with the courage of chronic poverty, expressed in a letter from Dublin on 14th November 1821: 'With my face prostrated upon the few square feet of soil that will cover my grave, I am invoking the shadow of Torquato, following whose example I try to fortify my heart against the anguish of poverty, but I foresee that, even poorer than that great spirit, I shall not find a pitiful hermit who will cover my ashes with a stone, nor write upon it: "Here lies Edmondo the Pilgrim".' And later on he begged Foscolo to take him on as his secretary, however small the salary.

Yet life's necessities were already pressing Foscolo while Angelini was sending his first begging letters. Urgent problems made Foscolo regret his departure for London: what demon had pushed him into such an adventure? And worse still, why had he departed without consulting or even taking leave of his *Donna Gentile* in Florence?

His meeting with Quirina had been the decisive factor in Foscolo's life. And as for Quirina, their encounter had transformed her life into a mission: to be the guardian angel of the restless poet. Quirina was not beautiful, was thirty-two years of age when she met the much younger Foscolo, and was in name only the wife of a very wealthy but impotent husband. Quirina had loved Foscolo deeply, from the day she had read *Le Ultime Lettere di Jacopo Ortis*: 'After that kiss I was made divine. My thoughts are now higher and more joyful, my heart is fuller of compassion . . .' For nine years of married life Quirina had lived between her house in Florence in the Via dei Servi and the farm of San Leolino, half-way between Florence and Montevarchi upon the Chianti hills, managing her own properties and those of her husband, until the day on which she first met Foscolo in Florence. From that day she undertook a mission of love and indulgence: to succour and suffer smilingly, to be the counsellor, the benefactrix, the custodian of Ugo's secrets, for ever and ever, *dum vivam et ultra.*

Foscolo had not immediately found Quirina very attractive. It was only when he was told that she was a friend of Alfieri's that he looked at her with some attention. But her agitation did arouse his curiosity, and he thought that it would be a mistake not to accept the love of this chaste married woman who was offering herself so humbly.

He had told her that he wanted his Quirina to be 'mild, biddable and honest'; and mild, biddable and honest Quirina was, happy to be so for him. And now, amidst the poverty and worries of London, the image of Quirina was emerging again. Quirina knew how to look into Ugo's life with clear and gentle eyes. Quirina loved Ugo just as he was, surrendering and forgetting herself to enable him to receive through her love and total dedication everything he needed for his spritual and material needs. For herself Quirina asked only the secret joy of perfect memories and a few of Ugo's thoughts, the giving of an hour of his time. She asked merely the happiness of knowing that he loved and was loved, without forgetting the woman who loved him so loyally, and had never betrayed him, and was satisfied with kissing his portrait.

So what was he doing in London? Why did he not return to the woman who would say: 'Ugo, you are my master, and I am your servant, your mother...'

But Quirina's company and great kindness, her anxiety to satisfy all his desires and needs, were not enough to clear away his worried thoughts. And his deeper thoughts remained a secret from Quirina.

IV

The first few months in London give the key to all the pain that increased as time passed. His pride and arrogance were raising a wall between what could be described as his two lives: the one that Quirina knew only too well, with its permanently dark future and his desperate fight to find enough money to exist; and the other life of putting up a good front before the world. In passing judgement upon the society that had received him with such warmth, only to let him drop when his poverty became all too evident, one must bear in mind that Foscolo's attitude on his arrival had been decidedly ill-advised.

His patrons in the eclectic society of London—a society always ready to receive an illustrious foreigner like a rare animal for the mere pleasure of showing him off to their friends—had been Lord and Lady Holland. In 1816 Holland House enjoyed a unique position in the high society of London. It was a picturesque manor about two miles from the city of that time, standing in a marvellous park. The house had been built in 1607 for Sir Walter Cope, and from him it had passed to his son-in-law Henry Rich, first Earl of Holland, and from him the house took its name. The Earl was twice a prisoner in his own manor, the first time in 1633 by order of Charles I for having challenged Lord Weston to a duel, and the second time by order of parliament for attempting to put Charles back on the throne, a crime for which the king himself was beheaded in 1649.

Holland House, however, after having been used by the Parliamentary General as his headquarters, was later given back to the Countess of Holland and in 1716, after the marriage of the Dowager Countess to the Earl of Warwick, passed to the celebrated essayist Joseph Addison, who died there in 1719. Around 1762 the manor was sold to Henry Fox, and his son Charles lived there when he was young.

The house was built like the letter H, with a splendid portal designed by Inigo Jones, and in recent years some elegant gates of wrough iron had been added. In the great hall there was a copy of the statue of Fox erected in Bloomsbury Square; and the many rooms were rich with gilded stucco and paintings by Parmigianino, Velasquez, Murillo and collections of lovely miniatures, sculptures and drawings by the old masters. The most impressive room was the library or Long Gallery, measuring 105 feet by 18 feet, and containing 18,000 books besides a rich collection of manuscripts and autographs. The gardens were magnificent and adorned with elegant buildings, the flowerbeds designed like coats of arms with Italian mottoes, and the park planted with rare, exotic trees. Holland House, already famous for the regal magnificence of Rich and later as a seat for the councils of Cromwell, was for nearly two centuries a centre for brilliant men and lovely women, painters and poets, philosophers and statesmen. It was by tradition a meeting place for the Whigs or Liberal Party, and the Hollands received not only high society but also the best known figures in the literary, philosophical and political worlds in England and other European countries. Lord Holland, always a champion of freedom, gave expression to his feelings by offering generous hospitality to victims in the cause of liberty. Moveover, Holland House was attracting men of many shades of opinion, for the master of the house and his wife had travelled a great deal, and their vast, if not really profound, knowledge of ancient and modern literature and their brilliant minds, as well as Lady Holland's elegance and Lord Holland's easy, attractive manners, combined to bring together the best intellects of that brilliant epoch.

When Foscolo arrived in London, the Hollands had just returned from a visit to Italy, where they had learned of Foscolo's fame, and remembered their old friendship with the Countess of Albany, dating back to their long stay in Italy in the early years of their marriage. Giuseppe Binda from Lucca, who had been a kind of financial secretary to the Hollands in Italy and was now resident librarian at Holland House, had met Foscolo in Florence, and glad to meet him again in London had spoken enthusiastically of him to the Hollands. Thus Foscolo had been, and remained till the May or June of 1817, a regular visitor to Holland House. His vivacious conversation was an ornament to the famous supper-room, and the spontaneous kindness of Lady Holland had at once made him a literary lion. Lord Holland always said, even when their relationship was becoming less friendly, that Foscolo was one of the greatest men he had ever met.

Foscolo himself had been amazed by the company at Holland

House. In the drawing-rooms of Milan and Florence he had met famous people, both Italians and foreigners; but they were superficial gatherings, with few signs of affluence, whereas Holland House appeared to him as a world of vast luxury. The receptions were always sumptuous, the *habitués* being Samuel Rogers, Sir James Mackintosh, Lord John Russell, Brougham, Jeffrey and Hallam. It was customary to pay a call at Holland House about dinner time, and as the dining-room was not particularly large, whenever a new guest arrived Lady Holland's voice would be heard: 'Listen, down there, make room for Samuel Rogers!' or whoever was the latest arrival. People ate elbow to elbow at the table, but the conversation was brilliant and most pleasant. The vast, rich library that Lord Holland had inherited and enlarged aroused Foscolo's enthusiasm and in those years when it was difficult to consult rare books, the courtesy with which Lord Holland placed his library at the disposal of his friends revealed him as a man full of sympathy for culture. The library was indeed a drawing-room-library, adorned with portraits of famous men, including one of Baretti by Sir Joshua Reynolds; the shelves were crammed with treasures from many countries and periods, and in that vast room Foscolo's eloquence and prodigious memory often sparkled. There he met his most eminent friends: the Duke of Bedford, Samuel Rogers, Roger Wilbraham, Lady Aberdeen, Lady Dacre, Lady Westmoreland, Lady Lyttleton— so many women among his friends!—all competing with one another to introduce him to other people and help him. There was no dinner or reception that he did not attend.

And Foscolo, during those first months, took great care to hide his financial situation. He was received as an equal, and he charmed everybody with his conversation and perfect manners.

In a letter written to Silvio Pellico the following year, Foscolo mentioned, not without pardonable vanity, those early, frail successes: 'To have a better knowledge of Latin and Greek helped me to reaffirm that little literary fame with which I met the English; and they put me severely to the test by asking me for interpretations of Greek passages to insert into some of their journals published expressly for classic literature, and for inscriptions to be placed upon monuments and statues.' What his suggestions and inscriptions were we do not know, but there remains a trace of one which was suggested by Foscolo to Lord Holland for the monument erected to his nephew Charles James Fox, leader of the Whig Party:

CAR. JAC. FOX
Cui plurimae consentiunt gentes
populi primarium fuisse virum.

In a letter dated 20th January 1817 Lord Holland wrote: 'What a beautiful inscription you have composed for me!' But a few days later he wrote again: 'In the second book *De Finibus* there are the same words as those that are in *De Senectute*, but three other *uno ore cui plurimae consentiunt gentes populi primarium fuisse virum*, and if we place in front of it "*Carolus Jacobus Fox—Uno ore cui*" etc. It would be, I think, a very suitable inscription.' From which one can see that Foscolo should have been more cautious with the erudite latinists when he was fishing in the ancient classics to compose an epitaph.

But Foscolo could not continue that kind of life for long. Anyone familiar with English society and the formality that ruled it then and continued till the Second World War—a formality that still survives among the older members of the aristocracy—is surprised that society should have tolerated Foscolo for such a long time: his strident voice, his gesticulations, his uncontrollable bursts of anger were in such strong contrast to the cool, quiet manners of the English, always moderate in their gestures and speech, always conversing softly, never contradicting one another, enjoying conversation suitable for a university, where everybody loved to hear other people's opinions without changing their own.

In the previous century Baretti had been able to adapt himself to the manners of a society that seemed wrapped in Chinese ceremonial; but Baretti was a Piedmontese, cold and rational, who had astutely understood that the English loved polemics expressed with spirit and grace, but only in books and other printed matter, while conversation in drawing-rooms or around a dinner-table should be formal and courteous. To every gentleman his own house was his little court.

But Foscolo never realised that he was an outsider, the very opposite of these people, and made the mistake of believing himself to be interesting because he was 'different'. It was a miracle that so many talented and cultured men and women gave Foscolo their sympathy, admiration and even friendship; naturally that kind of friendship that English people offer a foreigner, and which is always tinged with polite condescension.

Every celebrity had a frail and uncertain life in London society; a new arrival, especially if famous, was well received and attracted curiosity, was at times idolized like a god, but his success was very short lived, especially if his manners were deplorable or irritating. A celebrity's success might last if he produced new works worthy of praise, but Foscolo, alas, gave no sign that he was on the verge of giving birth to new poems or works. He talked incessantly in those early years of strictly literary plans, like the edition of the Italian Classics, or the *Letters*, but it was no more than talk, as was his effort to get a reprint of the *Jacopo Ortis*, a most lovely book, but alas, *déjà vu*. And from Italy, eagerly awaited, Cantos of Byron's *Don Juan* arrived regularly, and from Scotland Walter Scott, already knighted by the Prince Regent, was launching two or three highly popular historical novels every year. For the moment, there was nothing left for Foscolo but to retire into seclusion, and it was remarkable that so many people in society remembered his name.

On the other hand, what could that society do for him except flatter his vanity? It was a sad thing that Foscolo mistook that admission into the great world of Holland House for elevation to Mount Parnassus. He had, during his years in Milan, become so bitter that to find himself received as an equal in London by a rich and courteous English society made him lose his head. It gave him the most absurd idea of seriously believing that he must, at any price, appear a *gentleman* and live like one to retain the estimation and friendship of that society. His colossal error was in believing that people would have shown him the door if he had told them that he had to work for his living. From this foolish mistake stemmed all Foscolo's tribulations in London.

Foscolo made yet another mistake. At that time all the poets in Europe were trying to copy Byron's way of life. But Byron was a wealthy English peer, and his fertile mind allowed him continuously to produce poems which were ample and complete works, through which ran his philosophy and his satire of the English world. That was his great attraction for London society. Moreover, handsome Lord Byron was surrounded by an aura of fascination by his amorous scandals, one of them tinged with the wickedness of near-incest. How could Foscolo delude himself that he could copy Byron's life, when he was far from handsome, and did not possess the English poet's facile vein, and even less the means and resources to lead the life of Byron who in Italy, it was said (and it was true), was living like a lord in a palace on the Canal Grande with a host of servants and mistresses?

V

Two months after his arrival in London, Foscolo was utterly penniless and without resources, and he had also incurred some debts. At the end of November he had received from Zante £100 which had saved him. Another friend from the Ionian Islands, Giorgio Foresti, who was at that moment in London, had helped him with another £50; but in February of the following year Foresti was still asking urgently, in a letter to Calbo, for repayment.

There still remained his greatest anchor, and already in October Foscolo had written a somewhat pathetic letter to Quirina describing his miserable condition and prospects; his 'final destiny of going from house to house giving lessons in Italian, Greek and Latin to buy daily bread'. The tone of his letter was bitter and probably quite sincere, but it is painful to note that even in such a pathetic confession he had not been able to resist the theatricality of adding 'Greek and Latin'. To bring themselves to be teachers of Italian was the usual solution for nearly all Italian exiles, yet to Foscolo it meant giving up his social position; and did Foscolo really mean to do it? One may doubt it; and indeed he never did it, not even in the darkest days, and always preferred to await his fortune.

Nevertheless, the lack of money without the prospect of more caused him much anguish. To make matters worse, towards the end of February 1817 he suffered great pain in one of his legs; one doctor urged amputation but Rose, at that moment in London, insisted that he consult another physician, who succeeded in effecting a cure. But this meant increased expenditure and Rose, to whom Foscolo had opened his heart, advised him not to speak openly to his society friends, because in London it was a rule never to mention one's private affairs among gentlemen.

At last Foscolo understood that his pen was the sole means of earning his daily bread. He read a lot to become familiar with literary taste in England, and his first short published work was an article in

29

memory of Francis Horner, a Member of Parliament whom Foscolo had met at Holland House and who had died on 8th February 1817, at only thirty-one years of age. Foscolo translated Horner's parliamentary speeches into Italian, and published them in May that year, under the title *Discorsi nel Parlamento—on the death of Francesco Horner—translated from the English*. He dedicated the translation to Lord Holland's son, Henry, and the little work circulated among his society friends.

That spring a new edition of the *Jacopo Ortis* was also published, but this had unfortunate results as it involved Rose, Quirina and one of Rose's friends. The edition had been, in a certain sense, planted upon Foscolo by a London bookseller, Romualdo Zotti, who had published the book on his own initiative without Foscolo's consent, and there was nothing else for it but to revise the edition. The whole affair, however, seems strange, as a few weeks previously John Murray, famous as Byron's publisher, had already published the *Jacopo Ortis*; but Zotti had lent Foscolo £40, and when his edition of *Ortis* came out he refused to take responsibility for the sales, and asked Foscolo to reimburse the £40. Foscolo, in desperation, borrowed it from Rose who, not being rich and not having the cash available, borrowed it from a friend, with authority from Foscolo that if by Christmas he should not be in a position to repay the money, Rose, or Foscolo himself, should address themselves to the *Donna Gentile*. It so happened that Quirina, who had not heard from Ugo since the previous October, wrote to Rose for news begging him to give Foscolo, on her behalf, any monetary assistance he should need, so Rose answered Quirina's letter and told her of the loan. During 1817 Rose travelled to Italy 'to live more economically', and on 12th December he thanked Quirina for her offer to reimburse him the £40 but suggested she should wait until Christmas to give Foscolo time to do it himself. Alas, in March 1818 Quirina received a letter from Foscolo in which he expressed his surprise at Rose's urgency to recover the sum before the agreed time, which should have been December 1818, one year after the date mentioned by Rose in his letter. Quirina's faith in Foscolo was boundless, and she wrote to him that she was 'astounded at the wrong date of repayment, an error, no doubt, by Rose'. Anyhow, on 4th March 1818 Quirina repaid Rose the £40, for which he sent her a receipt. A messy business, alas, and tangled with unnecessary lies....

The English edition of the *Letters of Jacopo Ortis* was dedicated to the poet Samuel Rogers, whom Foscolo had met at Holland House. In the dedicatory letter Foscolo lamented that his heart was no longer what it had been in his youth, for it had suffered too much moulding by the world: 'Indeed out of respect for the world I dare to inscribe the edition in your name, instead of mine, except for a few copies that are accompanied by this letter, to tell you that the reading of the *Piaceri della Memoria* [a small work of Rogers] and the friendship that you have been good enough to show me add to the happier memories that I shall retain in the uncertain future.' The last sentence was almost prophetic, because the friendship with Samuel Rogers lasted through all the troubled years of Foscolo's life in London.

There was a reason for the editions with the dedication to Rogers being limited in number, because Foscolo dedicated other copies of his work to the many people who had been kind to him, with regrets that he should be reduced to offering the emotions and thoughts of his youthful years. The majority of those special copies he gave to ladies: Lady Lyttleton, Lavinia Spencer, Lady Charlotte Campbell, Lady Carysfort; and some of them thanked him most cordially and one, who signed herself H.F.R., wrote: 'How dear, how amiable is this Foscolo! I love Jacopo Ortis, dead or alive, but I love even more Ugo Foscolo, so it is a little lie to say that nobody loves him any more!'

But notwithstanding the gallant letters, troubles remained, indeed they were mounting up, and Foscolo could no longer hide his irritability. He even showed his annoyance in letters to English friends, and the state of his nerves in those months showed very clearly that he was on the point of a breakdown. Even Lord Holland complained of Foscolo's intolerance and his uncontrollable temper. His anger against the whole world became so annoying that people were saying: 'At Holland House they have had quite enough of Foscolo.'

The series of essays, *The Customs, Literature and Political History of Italy and England,* which the publisher John Murray had agreed to bring out, was abandoned, the reason being that Foscolo could not draw any immediate money. And the idea of publishing the Italian Classics in a subscribed edition was also dropped, partly because Murray was discouraged by Lord Guildford and partly because the publisher did not feel sure he could get a list of subscribers.

One heavy blow after another struck Foscolo in that very London which could still offer him some social enjoyment and intellectual advantage. He began to feel that it might be better for him to leave England; he thought of returning to the Ionian Islands, and wrote to Lord Guildford: 'My earnings do not permit me to face life in this country.' Lord Guildford was politically interested in the Ionian Islands and forced Foscolo to speak frankly, and with great tact and kindness induced him to accept a loan, which Foscolo accepted reluctantly, to put his affairs in order.

Another cruel event was the death of his beloved mother. Diamantina Spathis had been the embodiment of maternal love, and although most news of Ugo reached her indirectly, she always showed great affection for this tempestuous son. He received the news of his mother's death in a letter from his brother Giulio that reached him in May, one month after the event; and Ugo, who in the interval had written to her, felt ashamed at having done nothing to compensate for all the sacrifices she had endured for him. His grief was so great that it moved even his English friends. Lady Holland wrote him, in the purest Italian, a letter that was full of condolences and protestations of friendship, and invited him to spend a few days at Holland House before she and Lord Holland departed for the Continent.

To all his friends Foscolo announced that he was on the point of leaving London and returning to Greece. He wrote in July to Lord Holland who was in Brussels: 'My mother's death, breaking my heart with sadness and regret, condemns me to new worries. But so be it! I shall leave at the beginning of August.' He explained that he had decided to travel with the Ionian representatives who had come to London on 27th June to submit to the Prince Regent the new constitution of the Ionian Islands; and in his letter Foscolo begged Lord Holland to use his influence with the provisional government to secure for him some academic position, adding that he would be in Greece for the arrival of Lord Guildford, who was going there with an educational mission. Charles Fox was already there. Without his friends Foscolo was feeling lonely: 'I need to love and to be loved', he wrote to Lord Holland, 'and here I have neither relatives nor friends, and my poverty prevents me from taking a wife.' But the letter to Lord Holland ended with an affirmation of his deep sorrow in abandoning London where he had found so much cordial hospitality: 'Yet the fear of poverty and the sorrow at having to accept my friends' help has often troubled my days and nights.'

Lord Holland tried to raise Foscolo's spirits: 'All your friends in England will regret the loss of your always pleasant company, but none will be so selfish as to deplore your resolution if this proves to be for your good. You must finish your *Letters*, and not only the *Letters* but some other great work. The public and posterity are entitled to the intellectual enrichment enjoyed by all who had the chance to know you personally and enjoy your conversation. If you do not produce some great book it will be your fault, for you have the raw material, and you lack neither ardour nor inspiration to do it.'

He did not leave England, although he had announced his impending arrival in Florence to Quirina and the Countess of Albany. This was ostensibly because he could not obtain an English passport, but the real truth was that he had no desire to leave, and on 15th August he wrote frankly to Lady Flint: 'I felt my heart tearing to pieces at the mere idea of leaving England. Before knowing the English I thought that it was enough to have a high opinion of them; now I love them, and I thank the horse that nearly broke my leg for delaying my departure for Greece. There will be stronger reasons to make me remain at least the whole of this year.'

Lady Flint was one of those noble ladies to whom Foscolo gave, even by letter, a few lessons in the Italian language. There were also Lady Holland, Lady Carlotta Campbell with her two charming daughters whom Foscolo called 'the most gracious and dearest creatures that were ever modelled by the hand of Nature and adorned by education'. There were the three sisters Fitzgerald: Pamela, Lucia and Sophia, to whom, especially Pamela, Foscolo wrote charming little letters; and the daughters or nieces of Sir Roger Wilbraham, Giulia Luisa and Anna, with whom by word of mouth or in letters Foscolo delighted in exchanging arguments and disquisitions on love. There was Miss Wilmot, with whom he enjoyed talking about Petrarch and Homer and many other things. There were others too, and to his ample circle of women friends Foscolo confessed with a smile that he 'never succeeded in talking to ladies without introducing the subject of love'. There were, indeed, many reasons to induce him to remain in London. And, in his own mind, every woman meant romance.

With the coming of summer many of his English friends were leaving London for the usual visits to the Continent: Rose went, and so did Lord John Russell. In June the Hollands departed for Holland. In July Lady Campbell went to Italy with her daughters, carrying with her a letter of introduction to the *Donna Gentile*, in which Foscolo spoke of the warm friendship and consolation that Lady C. had expressed to him in his recent bereavement. He also gave letters of introduction to other friends.

In September he went off to the country. His cousin Dionisio Bulzo, who had come with the representatives of the Ionian Islands, had given him a pleasant sum of money, and with money in his hands Foscolo's horizon immediately became rosy and serene.

The country was only Kensington, at that time still open fields and orchards, but it was near Holland House, and there he could enjoy the splendid library. Moreover, a friend sent him a short letter on 17th September advising him that certain bankers were willing to discount a bill for him, and he could send at once to collect the money; and a few days afterwards Lady Westmoreland enclosed £50 in a letter with the kindly condition that he should not reimburse her until absolutely convenient to him. Money from his cousin Bulzo, money from the accommodating bankers, money from the kind lady: how could he ever think of leaving London? It was indeed the Garden of Eden.

He went therefore to Kensington to a small apartment to which he had his letters addressed: 'Hugo Foscolo Esquire, 19 Edward Square, Kensington, près de Londres'. Both square and house still exist. In his letters he mentioned that he had moved to 'a remote part of London'; but his financial affairs, rather more than his inclination for solitude, had prompted him to go out of town. He was giving up the pleasures of conversation 'because the fear of being tiresome to others would have made me tiresome to myself'; he was now living 'soberly and remote', and his sole distraction was 'to visit some friendly houses to watch people playing whist; but I go in and walk about without speaking a syllable . . .' Of course, now that the black humour caused by lack of money had evaporated, this talk of solitude was merely a pose.

Ugo Foscolo, in the portrait by Andrea Appiani in the Brera Academy in Milan.

The inscription that registers the translation of the body to Florence.

The poet's tomb in Chiswick Cemetery.

Page 173.

Name.	Abode.	When buried.	Age.	By whom the Ceremony was performed.
Ugo Foscolo * No. 1377.	Turnham Green	Sep. 18th 1827	50 Years	Henry Curtis Cherry Curate.
Aaron Charles Ashley No. 1378.	Strand on the Green	Sep. 19th 1827	6 Years	Thos. Horne B.D Officiating Minister
John Hopwood	Strand on the Green	Sep. 26th 1827	72 Years	Thos. Horne B.D Officiating Minister

BURIALS in the Parish of *Chiswick* in the County of *Middlesex* in the Year 18 27

Margin note: Exhumed by order of the Home Secretary June 9th 1871. Removed from Chiswick on the 10th 1871. Re-interred at Santa Croce Florence June 24th 1871.

The inscription of the poet's burial in the Parish of Chiswick register.

Application having been made to me the
Right Honble Henry Austin Bruce
One of Her Majesty's Principal Secretaries
of State, for permission to remove the body of
Ugo Foscolo
I do hereby, in virtue of the Powers vested in
me by the 23 sections of the . 18 & 21 Vict cap
51 grant License, for the removal of the body
of Ugo Foscolo
from
Chiswick Churchyard
on condition that the removal is effected with
due care and attention to decency early in the
morning and that Mc Dougall's disinfecting
Powder or Chloride of Lime, be freely sprinkled
over the Coffin, the Soil or any matter that
may be offensive

Given under my hand at Whitehall   H.A. Bruce
this 14th day of April 1870.—

The Home Office authorisation for the exhumation of the body.

John C. Hobhouse, historian and man of letters.

Lord Vassall Fox Holland, great patron of the poet.

Foscolo's tomb in Chiswick Cemetery.

n old print of Bohemia House, Turnham Green, where Foscolo died on 10 September 1827.

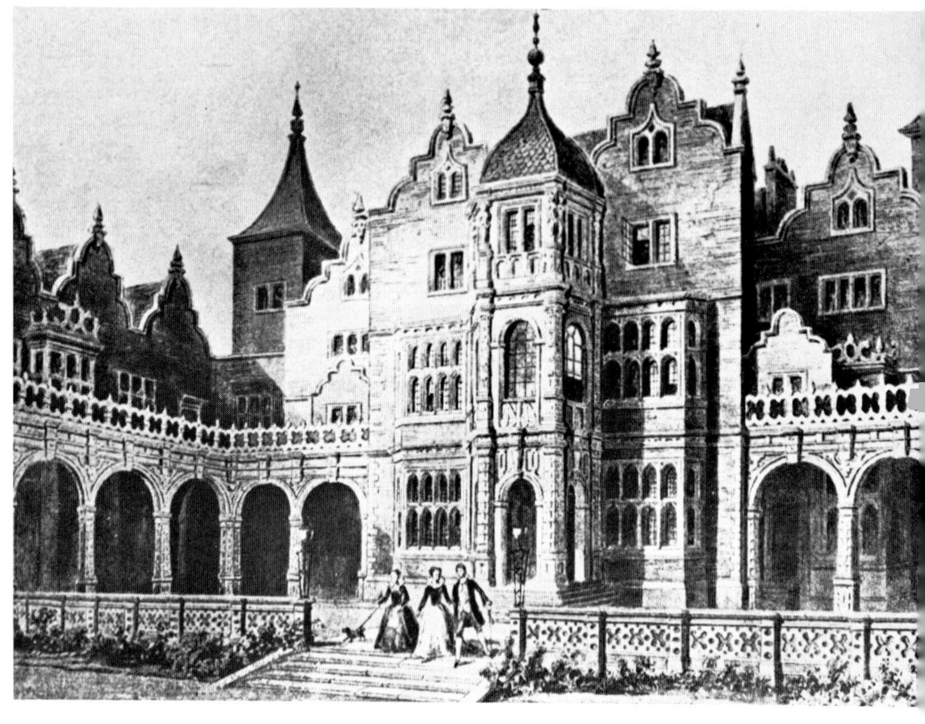

Holland House, the magnificent house of Lord and Lady Holland, the greatest cultural circle of time.

In Kensington he commenced work on the famous *Letters*, and sent the first to Lady Holland 'as ladies in matters of literary taste are wiser than scholars'. It was the letter that was published posthumously as a preface to the *Gazzettino del Bel Mondo*; and the few chapters and fragments of that Gazzettino are all that Foscolo composed of the famous *Letters* about which he had spoken so often at Holland House.

Nevertheless, he prepared the notes for an *Essay on Dante* for the *Edinburgh Review*; but that article went through many misadventures, until translated into English by Sir James Mackintosh, to whom it had been given by Jeffrey, the editor of the Review, who sent it to Dr Allen. It was not published till the following spring because the manuscript got lost and was retraced after Foscolo had already rewritten it with much trouble and irritation. That *Saggio su Dante* was, however, the start of a series of articles in the *Edinburgh Review* on the Italian Classics, and they brought Foscolo much praise.

In the quietude of Kensington the bitterness of life seemed to cease. The first letter from England was declared by Lord Holland *'de toute beauté, sévère et claire'*.

After a short while he returned to town, to rooms at 22 Woodstock Street, which was a more central address, and not expensive; and those rooms he kept for a long time.

In the meanwhile, Quirina in Florence was awaiting Foscolo's return, but weeks became months, and still no word came from London. At long last Quirina wrote herself, pouring out upon the page all her disappointment and her own loneliness. Nothing, she wrote to Foscolo, could change her love for him: 'Remember that you do not have any other mother than myself; I take this name with bashful pride, and from this moment I feel delighted, hoping that my son will not find the tender and anxious attentions of his mother unpleasant.' Quirina's love was at once splendid and pathetic. Like all women when they are deeply in love, she felt for her beloved not only passion but a maternal emotion, the anxious vigilance of a mother for her child; but alas, Quirina was not a beautiful woman. Worse still, she could not be a social ornament for Foscolo.

Indeed, he let two months go by before answering that moving letter, replying at last on 20th February 1818:

'I was silent, forced to it by affliction and desperation. I did not know what to say or not to say. Being unable to comfort you, I did not have the courage to reveal my troubles nor the strength to dissimulate them. And yet I felt and still feel very often at night a bitter regret; but you know me—too much heart is worse than too little. The excess of misfortune makes one dumb, and perplexity prevents one from reaching a decision, and when one cannot take a decision, one can but lie in the inactivity of death. I wrote to you that I would be passing through Florence. I had everything ready, and then I was invited by Bulzo to ride with him. The horse threw me and I broke a leg, the same leg that had barely recovered from the rheumatism of previous months. I was unable to travel, and Bulzo departed alone. He helped me, however; but what help can be enough when each visit by the surgeon costs one guinea, that is five *scudi*? I recovered, and went into the country to hide my poverty, for here poverty is a shame that no merit can wash away; it is a crime cruelly persecuted by the world. The wise men of this country consider me an oracle, and one of their papers said that I was the greatest genius they had ever met. You must realize that here the newspaper articles are written by rich and noble people, but poverty would make even Homer despicable in their eyes. Would to God I could write in English! Who can read my Italian? The publishers tell me that you may sell fifty copies of an Italian book in three years, while an English book by a good author will sell five or six thousand copies in two or three weeks. You see, therefore, that I could get rich if I had a translator! In the meantime I have written a book about Italian literature. They had promised me the moon, glory, readers and more. . . . I worked till I ruined my health; then I wrote articles for magazines, writing in French so as to help the translators. And I would not dare to have such things coming out with my name. So have pity on me. . . .'

In the end, he told Quirina that he was hoping to obtain a passport that would put him under English protection, and be able to return to Florence: 'I will come on foot, even if I fall down along the way. . . .'

But why write such boastful words about being a great genius? And why try to justify his inability to produce nothing more than a few magazine articles? Perhaps he felt that in London his poetical vein had dried up, and was angry at seeing himself reduced to dashing off contributions for reviews, things so much below the standard of his poetry, and in particular that poem *Le Grazie* that was awaiting completion and would never be completed.

Again the words that he wrote to Quirina in a following letter on 3rd March seem as if spoken to himself:

'Yours of 13th February reached me last night. I am now writing before going to bed, as the post is collected at midday; and the hours pass sadly, without consolation or harmony, all the hours of my miserable life. Last year I was astounded by the noise of the great world; it was then necessary to be known; now it is necessary that I should hide away. Now the days are all alike for me; I no longer see rich people who would make me feel my extreme poverty, nor do I wish to annoy them by showing it. But mine is a *'violenta e disperata pace'*; and writing to you I do not need to dissimulate it. Indeed, Quirina, I feel as if I were living upon a deserted rock in the middle of an ocean, in an unremitting storm, and I see the waves coming to submerge me, and I struggle; and only the shame of impending and imminent infamy prevents me from throwing myself into the sea . . .'

And once again he ends the letter:

'I am contemplating returning to Florence, for nothing else but to die there . . .'

Did Quirina really believe all this nonsense? A strange contradiction to this 'dramatic' state of things appears, on the other hand, in a letter to Lady Flint, in which Foscolo describes himself as feeling his 'very soul turned out at the idea of having to leave England', and thanking the horse that, by breaking his leg, delayed his departure . . . At the same time he was writing to Quirina that he 'was 'praying to the Gods that Thomas Grenville could obtain for him an English passport that would give him the happiness of living in peace in Florence with his *Donna Gentile*'.

And Quirina, a woman of great common sense even if full of love for her Ugo, replied laughing at his imaginary difficulties in the way of returning to Florence: 'Any passport would be good, and no one in Florence would oppose your return', and promised she would provide him all the money for travelling expenses.

But Foscolo's real desire was the one expressed to Lady Flint: to live, of course, in peace and happiness, in England. London had already worked upon Foscolo the magic that so many other exiles were to experience after him: London was a hard and pitiless Circe, who did not grant her boons very easily, and one had to earn them at the price of sweat and blood; but London seduced every exile, and no one could say why.

Callirrhoe

I

The success of the two articles published by the *Edinburgh Review* (the second, *Observations on the Originality of Dante's Poems*, appeared in September) and the £32 received for the first, double what had been agreed, prompted Foscolo to anticipate immediately an income of £300 a year, merely upon the hope of being invited to write further contributions. The planned edition of the Italian Classics discarded by John Murray was now being discussed again, and Foscolo thought it would earn him £10,000, a fabulous sum. Of course it was only on paper, but to the optimistic Foscolo every plan became immediate reality. He intended to publish the great Italian poets with their biographies and the history of their times plus his critical notes, making altogether thirty-two volumes. He could see them already on the shelves of innumerable readers, and so convinced was he that he wrote to Quirina to find him a new secretary-copyist to take the place of the faithless Calbo. Foscolo, the man who proclaimed himself sceptical in spiritual matters, was most credulous in the things pertaining to real life. He believed that it was enough to plan a book to become rich; from the moment the idea was being considered, he was inclined to spend the wealth that might never arrive.

On the wings of such stupendous projects, helped also by the splendid summer sun, Foscolo wrote to Pamela, one of the three daughters of Lord Edward Fitzgerald, who was then living in Thames Ditton, asking her to find him a small country house, as his heart was seeking peace in the country and he wanted to put the finishing touches to his beloved poem *Le Grazie*.

Pamela Fitzgerald found him a house in East Molesey for the modest rental of £84 a year. With his unique ability in financial acrobatics, Foscolo purchased furniture, house-linen, silver and all the ornaments for an elegant small house. He also bought a carriage and horses.

The source of these unexpected riches was an agreement made at that time with John Cam Hobhouse, whom he had met in the house of his great friend and admirer, the octogenarian Sir Thomas

41

Wilbraham, a great lover and student of Italian. He lived in Twickenham, another picturesque village not far from East Molesey, famous
for the home, still preserved, of the great poet Alexander Pope, who
in the lovely garden of his house on the shores of the Thames had
erected a 'grotto' that still attracts visitors.

Hobhouse had recently returned from Venice, where Foscolo's
name was still remembered, and he went to Twickenham to meet
the celebrated poet of the *Sepolcri*. His sympathy was increased when
he heard that the poet had to struggle to earn his living, and at once
offered to help him. It so happened that Hobhouse was on the point
of publishing his notes about the Fourth Canto of Byron's *Childe
Harold*, and he and Byron had both decided to include in the
Appendix a brief history of the state of Italian literature at that
time. But the preparation of an adequate survey was beyond them,
and the meeting with Foscolo appeared to Hobhouse a splendid
opportunity to find out from the most brilliant critic of Italian
literature what they wanted to know.

Hobhouse felt that he might as well ask Foscolo to write the
history of the revolutions in Italy, and certainly no one was better
suited than Foscolo to narrate the last days of the Regno Italico, since
he had been one of the Viceroy of Italy's soldiers and had taken part
in those events.

According to Foscolo's notes written later about that rather
complex matter, Hobhouse, who had a contract with an English
publisher for £2,500, would have paid Foscolo £50 a month, and
he would give him another £400 when the work was completed.
This would take a full year; hence the fantastic expenses incurred by
Foscolo for his house at East Molesey.

His stay there began very pleasantly. The Fitzgeralds were nearby,
and with his small carriage Foscolo could visit the Wilbrahams and
keep in touch with his London friends. The summer of 1818 had
brought him the friendship of Federico Confalonieri, who had come
to England to purchase some inventions which, it was said, would
revolutionise the world; some ships' engines, one to produce gas for
an entire house, and machines for weaving silk and wool. Confalonieri was full of enthusiasm for the good that would result to his
land in Lombardy, far from imagining that one day the Austrians
would condemn him to imprisonment in the Spielberg. Foscolo

and Confalonieri became friends, and together enjoyed that lovely mild English summer. Their last meeting was to be at the Hotel Sablonnière in London; but unfortunately Foscolo missed the appointment, and could not give Confalonieri his own letters for Italy.

The truth was that the work for Hobhouse was not progressing as fast as Foscolo had hoped, and after a few months he found that life in the country was becoming oppressive and too lonely. From Florence on 1st September Quirina proposed a meeting at Calais, but Foscolo replied: 'My Quirina, do come to Calais, and I will meet you there and escort you to England, to this hermitage where I have everything except a person that loves me. In other words I have nothing but loneliness, and am often desperate. If you would stay with me some little time, even only a couple of weeks, I should feel reborn, and I would do more work in a day than I do now in a month. Do come, as soon as you can, and you will find everything ready to welcome you, and my heart waiting for you alone.'

But Quirina could not leave so suddenly; and no sooner had his work helped Foscolo to get rid of his depression, than Hobhouse, at the beginning of December, gave him the terrible news that he could not possibly continue the arrangement he had made with Foscolo. He had uselessly spent £50,000 trying to be elected to the Commons for the Westminster constituency, and now there remained no other solution but to go most urgently to France to save money, and this he did at the beginning of the following year. A serious quarrel resulted, for Foscolo's nerves were again severely strained, and the destruction of all his hopes of financial peace by his arrangement with Hobhouse, which had prompted him to sign numerous little bills now getting near their settlement date, made him lose all control and sense of proportion. Hobhouse, who was a perfect gentleman, did all he could to placate Foscolo, but as the latter also had to pay the rent on his London rooms he signed more bills and sold, for a bargain price, many of his books and the silver he had bought for the Molesey house: better a mountain of promissory notes than the debtors' prison!

A Miss Murry helped him by paying the £14 rent for the rooms in London, and Hobhouse settled the most urgent of the bills. Touched by this gesture, Foscolo wrote him a letter full of gratitude.

II

He returned to the two rooms in Woodstock Street, but did not remain there long because he 'could not receive a single person, for they were too mean'. There, however, he was able to prepare the articles for the reviews, and as soon as possible, having hidden his poverty from his English friends, he moved to number 154 New Bond Street, where he once more put into practice his theory of appearing as a gentleman of means, a theory, he said, that was indispensable to success in their field of letters in England.

His real mistake was applying this theory in an excessive way; and the rumours that reached Italy about the tone and style of his elegant and luxurious way of life induced people to believe that Foscolo was gaining sums never heard of in Italy for his writings. Professor Philarete Charles of the Collège de France, who met Foscolo in 1819, broadcast a description of his residence that must have left people in Milan and Florence speechless. Everything was classic and pagan, with an Apollo in the sitting-room, and a Jupiter in the entrance hall. A portable altar served as a chimney piece, and Foscolo jokingly apologised for being dressed in modern clothes.

Where did he find the means to live in such style? The question was relevant since his letters to Quirina during that period were in complete contrast to the incredible rumours circulating in Florence about his luxurious way of life. In March 1819 he had described to Quirina his misadventures with Hobhouse, as usual exaggerating them: 'Of the thousand pounds that I was expecting in one year I only received one hundred, so that I was compelled to leave my little country house, though I still pay the rent, and I am living in London as best I can in two small rooms in Woodstock Street, where I would be ashamed to receive anyone.'

And poor Quirina, for whom Ugo's words were gospel, was very perplexed. She set in motion some cautious enquiries to ascertain the truth; and Leopoldo Cicognara, who visited London in 1819, informed her:

'Your friend is working at full stretch. When I arrived in London he had a horse, a carriage, a house in the country and rooms in town, and a servant. This was perhaps a little too much, and I think that he recognized it himself, and now his situation has slightly improved by taking a splendid apartment and furnishing it with good taste. This, of course, has cost him plenty of money; but I think that there is more comfort than distress, although he could easily have saved several hundred pounds by living more moderately. I tell you this merely to clarify your friend's situation.'

He added that the poet was keeping an interesting housekeeper, not very beautiful, but interesting. Foscolo considered her necessary to keep himself in good health. 'Consequently I do not consider his situation as needing such help as might come from a delicate and friendly hand.'

Besides, Foscolo was working hard at his articles and the ever-hoped-for editions of the Classics. But Cicognara, in his letter, had also mentioned the strange vagaries of Foscolo's mind, his mad fantasies, his sudden fears and fits of melancholy: 'and at times ideas of grandeur seem to exalt him.' All this enabled Quirina to form a correct diagnosis of Foscolo's condition, and she wrote to him begging him not to let his new love take him away from his old friends, of whom she was the most devoted.

It is not clear who Foscolo's new love might be: but Quirina, with the heart and mind of a deserted mistress, had judged correctly. She knew that Foscolo was continually passing through phases of adoration of this or that woman, and by the end of the year Foscolo had indeed conceived the idea of making a brilliant marriage.

III

Late in 1818 Foscolo had made the acquaintance of the family of Sir Henry Russell of Swallowfield, a former judge in Bengal, now pensioned. The Russells were living in Wimpole Street, and soon Foscolo found himself at home with this hospitable family full of young people—the judge had six sons and five daughters. Their mother, Lady Russell, had died four years previously. At first Foscolo was much attracted by Catherine, who was already married, but later he turned his thoughts to her sister Caroline, and for two years he loved her with the usual crescendo of his romantic ardour. The Russells were always sending him invitations and little notes enquiring about his health, and asking what diet would be suitable for him. These notes were nearly always written by Caroline. Foscolo used to escort her and her sisters, Rose and Henrietta, to receptions in other friends' houses, and soon Foscolo found himself so intimate with Caroline and one of her sisters that he took to reading Petrarch to them.

Caroline was a young lady full of common sense, honest and straightforward, with a gravity that was quite exceptional in such a young woman. But she had all the freshness of youth, and was full of grace and spirit. Foscolo fell in love with her, and as with him romance must always be pursued to its limits, he was soon madly in love. It never occurred to him that she might not feel the same; he forgot his forty years of age and his poverty. He was once again the poet of the letters of *Jacopo Ortis*.

Moreover, Foscolo was always in need of love to make him get down to work. If it was not poems and tragedies, it was love letters: great works of art themselves, written and rewritten and finally copied on fresh paper. He put into his love letters the same talent and poetic inspiration that he put into his poetry, driven by the same demon. And since his youth women had always sought him out, eager and pleased to tame this romantic poet and wandering, suicidal man, forever killing himself, but only in words. He committed suicide in his letters, in his imagination, and felt that his suicide had

47

indeed been consummated.

Could Foscolo, the ardent Foscolo, who in Italy had collected so many feminine admirers, reconcile himself to failing to conquer also the proud, perhaps frigid daughter of Albion? Pride and vanity had always been the prologue to all his love affairs.

First he made friends with Caroline's sisters and brothers. One of the secrets of his success in reaching the object of his love was to win the affection of the rest of the family first. The sisters, even the mothers of his mistresses had always been in love with him.

Caroline Russell had four sisters: Anne, Catherine, Henrietta and Rose Aylmer. Anne was married, and Foscolo met her briefly once. Of the six brothers, Charles soon became a close friend, and it was he who later translated into English a part of the *Essays on Petrarch*. Three other brothers were in India, and a fourth one, George, was still at school.

In 1924, three years before the centenary of Foscolo's death, a copy of the *Jacopo Ortis* was discovered in an Edinburgh bookseller's shop. The edition was the one published by Murray in 1817, and the two little volumes were beautifully bound into one volume in red morocco, and on the book-plate was the following dedication: 'To the Kind Damsel/Enrichetta Russell/Ugo Foscolo/Sincerely D.' And underneath, in ink in Foscolo's hand:

To Miss Henr. Russell
Ugo Foscolo
Wimpole Street 17th March 1819
Come andrà l'alma mia gioiosa e paga,
Se impunemente esser potrai si vaga?
Ippolito Pindemonte

Alas, Foscolo's purse was not brimming with money when he paid that costly homage to Henrietta Russell, for the very day before he had written to his *Donna Gentile* recounting the tragedy of his shattered hopes of collaborating with Hobhouse. Why, then, one feels compelled to ask, why this duplicity with Quirina, revealing his true situation and hiding from her the life of luxury that he was leading perhaps with the purpose of keeping up appearances with the Russells in the hope of becoming a son-in-law? Did he not feel a sense of shame when the answer arrived from Quirina enclosing practical help?

The Petrarch readings lasted a few months. Foscolo implanted in them something of Jacopo Ortis, and he did not notice, or did not want to notice, that his feelings were not returned. Indeed, having composed, according to the fashion of the time, such a famous epistolary romance, he resorted to letters to court Caroline. To one in which Foscolo reproached her for not believing that a new fire had entered his heart to warm it, Caroline replied that she preferred to consider that letter as never having been written. Foscolo persisted; Caroline replied that he should not delude himself with the hope that she shared his feelings, to avoid disappointment. She wrote it separately on a small sheet of paper, and Foscolo returned it to her saying that it was certainly not addressed to him. He had no fear of being disappointed, because he had never nourished any hopes; he no longer had a place in this world; the world could no longer offer him a home; it was enough for him to traverse this world and go to rest elsewhere.

In the spring of 1819 he was by now a constant visitor to the Russell house, and during those months he composed, to read to Caroline, his *Notes on Petrarch*, a work of true love that produced those *Saggi sul Petrarca* on which Foscolo's reputation in England mainly rests.

Sir Henry Russell, with the calm, sure eye of a judge, saw that in the poetry readings of his inflammable Greco-Italian friend there was something much warmer than mere academic teaching, and one day he told Foscolo: 'Be careful, my friend, for Caroline will make you lose your head.'

But the danger was reciprocal; it was Foscolo who, although deeply in love himself, was dreaming of making the lovely Caroline fall in love with him. And Caroline herself, who was twenty years younger than Foscolo, although not encouraging him, did not discourage him and found it decidedly amusing to be the object of the growing passion of the romantic Italian poet. The flirtation continued until Caroline left London.

In the summer of 1819 several friends of the Russells left for Switzerland, and Caroline went to Lausanne where one of her sisters was convalescing. Foscolo obtained permission to write to her, and from the drafts of those letters it is possible to understand that Caroline Russell must have found them quite different from the letters she was expecting from the poet. The author of *Jacopo Ortis* was an adept in the art of composing love letters, and in the notes to the departed friend he evoked her image, her voice, the very words that she used, seeking in those words meanings and intentions that were never there. For some of these letters Foscolo wrote two or even three drafts, seeking more suitable words to convey his feelings. He invented, in fact, a Caroline entirely different from the one who in Lausanne would have to read those exaggerated hymns of love.

Caroline lengthened her stay in Switzerland. And Foscolo kept writing to her things that must have alarmed her. And when, several months afterwards, Caroline returned, she told him in very plain words that he was mistaken.

Nor can one say that Caroline Russell had refused Foscolo's love and his strange offer of marriage out of sheer pride or disdain of a poor poet: nor was Foscolo such as to give the impression of being a man of humble birth. Caroline Russell was a young, sensible English lady, and although attracted by the famous poet who had read and commented on Petrarch with such fire and eloquence, she felt that marriage with him would be folly, and that the world would think so too. When Foscolo refused to believe her, she withdrew into a dignified reserve, and Foscolo's ardour passed all bounds.

The letters from Caroline to Foscolo no longer exist, because Foscolo returned them to Caroline on the tragic day that brought the end of all his hopes, and Caroline probably destroyed them. Foscolo, however, kept the drafts of his own letters, all written in French, perhaps thinking to use them some day as a new romance in the Ortis manner.

Foscolo wrote a letter to Caroline on 16th May 1820, his thirty-second in reply to Caroline's twelfth. The date of Caroline's return was approaching, and Caroline felt it necessary to make quite clear to Foscolo the uselessness of his persistence. Foscolo, for his part, suggested that he would reduce his visits to Wimpole Street gradually so that his absence, after Caroline's return, would not be noted.

But as soon as Caroline returned in October, Foscolo ran to Wimpole Street. From that moment things moved towards a crisis, and on 17th November he called to force Caroline to declare herself. There was a tempestuous scene and Caroline, compelled by the poet to express herself in unequivocal terms, told him plainly that there was no hope.

Yet, not even after this scene did Foscolo have the tact to keep away for even a short while; a few days later he begged her sister Henrietta to do him the favour of returning to Caroline the bundle of letters that she had written to him. Henrietta told him that Caroline had never been in love with him; and Foscolo, convinced that Henrietta would repeat the conversation to Caroline, told her: '*Je la perdrai en lui laissant le remords de ma destruction.*'

On the following Tuesday he presented himself again at Wimpole Street. It was early in the morning, and Foscolo did not realize that it was very bad manners to pay a visit at such an early hour. He found Caroline coming down the stairs already dressed to go out. Women, especially when they are not in love, are more resentful of theatrical scenes than men, and Caroline lost her patience. Foscolo wrote later: 'I saw you in your riding dress, with your green veil. On your pale face I could read your contempt, your coldness, and cruelty; your hands, that during our separation I had seen in my dreams, and one month before had believed I could touch and kiss, those very same hands seemed to me to be dripping with my heart's blood.'

Beautiful words, in the manner of Jacopo Ortis, but absurd; and there is a right moment for words of love. Caroline Russell certainly treated him badly. Yet, some weeks afterwards, Foscolo decided to make excuses, and after having drafted a letter five times, sent it on 1st January together with a fine copy of Tasso's *Aminta*. Caroline answered the same day thanking him, and the humble style of Foscolo's letter prompted her to say that he could return now and then to visit herself and her family. Foscolo replied to Henrietta in a letter which stated that he could not possibly return. But on 11th January he sent a long letter to Caroline intended to be 'the conclusion' of his love for her. The letter appears quite grotesque, and ends: 'Here, Madame, you have my delusions at which you may laugh at your ease.'

Of that love story for Caroline Russell there remains only one really lyrical page: the *Ode to Callirrhoe* that Foscolo enclosed in the copy of his *Essays on Petrarch* for Caroline Russell, an edition of only sixteen copies. If it is true that poetry is always the fruit of the soul's deep feelings, that invocation to the disdainful Callirrhoe was the last bloom to flower from that 'indefinable pathos that induces a gentle melancholy'. And from that day Foscolo must have sought a great deal of pathos at the fount of poetry to refill each day the bitter chalice of his life.

Did Foscolo really love Caroline Russell? Perhaps more in his mind than in his heart; and perhaps losing her wounded his vanity more than his heart. And perhaps—and we must remain in the field of suppositions for lack of documentation—perhaps more than anything else he felt the disappointment of seeing his great hopes of a good marriage go up in smoke. Strangely enough, Caroline Russell was the only woman whom Foscolo actually considered as a 'bride': all the other women were other men's wives. As for Quirina, even if she had been free to marry him, Foscolo would not have married her, for his vanity would have prevented him. Sad to say, his vanity was the main cause of his megalomania and of all his follies in England, and made him consider poor Quirina, the only woman who loved him with pure and total devotion, too modest, too housewifely, too provincial for him to take as his wife and introduce her to his London friends. The invitation to a visit of 'two weeks' that he had mentioned in the offer to meet her at Calais and bring her to London shows most clearly that he had no desire to attach himself to Quirina in the presence of his illustrious and noble friends at Holland House.

Caroline Russell, on the other hand, had appeared to him the ideal wife: she was a young lady of good family, with a splendid mind and education, from a rich family and well connected; with her he would have found the social and literary road to success open, in the fashion of that time, and his constant dream. To offer her his hand, as he had done in his last letter, to escort her to Florence where 'she would have been by no means the last person in wealth, but one of the first because of her name', were nothing but fine words, and one is prompted to say that it was a subconscious ray of common sense that made him add as a conclusion: 'Here, Madame, you have my delusions at which you may laugh at your ease.'

Nevertheless, his sorrow was great, and after four months it was still with him. And Foscolo poured it out to Quirina, and also to Mrs Wilmot—who was now Lady Dacre—to whom he wrote one of his last letters in the Jacopo Ortis style: 'I have lost my sleep at a moment when I indeed needed to find eternal sleep. For all this I blame my own folly, and my folly stemmed not only from the delusion that I knew the human heart, but also from my trusting nature which caused me to place the same trust in other people.'

Little by little he resumed his connections with the Russell family, though not as intimately as before. At the end of April there appeared a private edition of the *Essays of Petrarch*, printed by S. R. Bentley. Foscolo sent a copy to Charles Russell with a charming letter: 'The first idea of this commentary came to my mind one evening when I was reading some passages of Petrarch in your house, and I have now printed it so that it will remain in your family as a memento of the hospitality that your family gave to a foreigner, and which sooner or later will remain only as a memory. And as you turned part of it into English and revised what I ventured to write in your language, I feel that my dedication belongs to you.'

Afterwards he sent copies to the sisters Henrietta and Rose Aylmer. As Caroline felt that she was being left out, she sent the author a message that she too would welcome a copy. And Foscolo, who probably had recourse to this ruse to tempt the stubborn woman once again to resume the correspondence interrupted since January, sent her a special copy in which the essays were preceded by a dedication in verse to which he added a letter in French: '*Toutefois, puisque vous êtes dans le secret de mes illusions—puisque la Dédicace formait une condition essentielle de la promesse, et je vous ai dit que les vers étaient preparés, je les ai supprimés dans toute l'édition, hormis dans votre exemplaire et dans le mien . . . après la page 164 devant les poésies grecques vous y trouverez la date d'un jour qui a contribué à me faire croire sincèrement à l'existence réelle de Callirrhoe.*'

But Foscolo made the mistake of also sending the novelette *Adolphe*, with annotations that greatly irritated Caroline; and she brusquely broke off any further exchange of letters: 'I do not know why you sent me *Adolphe*; you know that I have already read it and I have not forgotten it. Do you wish me to take it as a sign that, with the shadows of night, the shadows of your heart have not disappeared? Do you think it generous that words spoken without special meaning should live so long in your memory?'

TO CALLIRRHOE

At Lausanne

> Her face was veil'd. Yet to my fancied
> sight
> Love, sweetness, goodness in her per-
> son shined.
> But oh!—I wak'd.
>
> Milton

I twine, far distant from my Tuscan grove,
The lily chaste, the rose that breathes of love,
The myrtle leaf and Laura's hallow'd bay,
The deathless flowers that bloom o'er Sappho's clay;

For thee Callirrhoe!—Yet by Love and years
I learn how Fancy wakes from joy to tears;
How Memory pensive, 'reft of hope, attends
The Exile's path, and bids him fear new friends.—

Long may the garland blend its varying hue
With thy bright tresses, and bud ever-new
With all Spring's odours; with Spring's light be drest,
Inhale pure fragrance from thy virgin breast!

And when thou find'st that Youth and Beauty fly
As heavenly meteors from our dazzled eye,
Still may the garland shed perfume, and shine
While Laura's mind and Sappho's heart are thine.

Strawberry Hill, 26th April 1820.

A CALLIROE

A Losanna

> Velato il viso. Ell'avea;—ma all'esta-
> tico mio sguardo
> Amor, bontà, dolcezza in sua persona
> Splendeano,—Ahimè, mi ridestai!...
>
> Milton

Intreccio, lontano dal mio etrusco boschetto,
il casto giglio, la rosa spirante amore, il ramoscello
di mirto e la sacra fronda di Laura,
i fiori immortali che spuntano sul cenere di Saffo:

Per te, Calliroe!... Ma dall'Amore e dagli anni
apprendo come la Fantasia passa destandosi dalla gioia
al pianto; come, pensosa e nuda di speranza,
la Memoria segue i passi dell'Esule, e lo avverte
di paventar nuovi amici.

Possa la mia ghirlanda mischiare per lungo tempo
le varie sue tinte alle tue lucide trecce, e rifiorire
sempre nuova con tutti gli olezzi di primavera!
Si vesta della luce di primavera, aspiri pure fragranze
dal virgineo tuo seno!

E quando vedrai che giovinezza e beltà fuggono
come celesti meteore dai nostri occhi abbagliati,
possa ancora la ghirlanda spander profumo e luce,
affinché vivano in te la mente di Laura, e il cuore di Saffo.

IV

The *Essays on Petrarch* were the finest fruit of Foscolo's intellectual life in exile. At twenty, the disappointment of his love for Isabella Roncioni had provided the inspiration for the *Jacopo Ortis*, and now still trembling with exalted passion, Foscolo with his false hope of conquering Caroline Russell—and it is noteworthy that his two best creations both flowered from amorous delusions—was inspired to produce the *Essays on Petrarch*. '*Per te, o Calliroe, lontano dal mio Etrusco boschetto intreccio il casto giglio, la rosa spirante amore, il ramoscello di mirto e la sacra fronda di Laura, i fiori immortali che spuntano sul cenere di Saffo.*'

It is worth remembering the genesis of these essays. Since 1818, when he had published in the *Edinburgh Review* the *Essay on Dante*, Foscolo had promised Jeffrey, the editor of the review, to follow it with similar studies upon the poetry of Petrarch and his period. In June and August 1819 Jeffrey reminded him of his promise, but only in December was the manuscript delivered. The editor delayed publication, and not until March did he send Foscolo a fee of £50, announcing that the essay would be published in the May issue. But Foscolo was impatient to see the essay come out, and arranged for a private edition of eight copies only, hoping to make a welcome gift to Caroline Russell. It was only the first essay, and on 10th March he sent two copies to Gino Capponi telling him: 'Do keep one in memory of your friend, and send the other to Lausanne as urgently and safely as you can, writing in clear letters (not as you usually do): 'To Mlle Caroline Russell, etc.'. In the event Capponi could not get the copy safely to Lausanne.

Foscolo was somewhat dissatisfied with the translation, a translation which he called 'frozen', as he had written to Capponi: 'Probably the text will appear stilted, larded with things that are not mine, and further doctored in the magazine issue that should appear any week', that is to say in May, 1820. But the essay did not appear in May even in a butchered version, and on 1st August Jeffrey apologized, with the excuse of having had to publish more urgent

57

articles that could not wait, and had taken up more space than had been foreseen. Foscolo, bitterly offended, broke his connections with the *Edinburgh Review*.

Fortunately Murray, who in London had realized Foscolo's annoyance, had hastened to purchase the entire MS of the *Essays on Petrarch*, giving Foscolo a fee more than double the one already paid by Jeffrey, sending it with the most courteous letter: 'I enclose 100 guineas, if this sum is sufficient to buy your essay, and believe me, I have never made a payment with greater satisfaction than this to a writer that I esteem so highly.' But when in April 1821 the article appeared, Foscolo was greatly disappointed, and made his outburst in a letter to Lady Dacre: 'The editor has altered and patched up my text so much that reading it in print I could no longer understand what I had written. In this kind of work, I can compare myself to a horse reduced to following the footmarks of a bull.'

Whether or not it was the fault of the translation, the essay as published by Murray in the *Quarterly* aroused no enthusiasm. Nobody congratulated either the author or the publisher. Indeed one reader by the name of Taylor wrote at length to the editor, adding: 'I should be grateful if you would pass my notes to the author.' Murray sent the letter on to Foscolo, who was doubly hurt, as the remarks referred to things produced neither from his pen nor from that of the translator.

In the meantime Foscolo, who was congenitally inclined to complicate affairs with two editors or printers without their knowledge, as he had already done with the *Jacopo Ortis*, arranged for a private edition of all the *Essays on Petrarch* with Bentley of Dorset Street in London, without revealing the serialization that John Murray had already begun in his review, clearly as a prelude to the publication in book form of the essays under the imprint of John Murray. And on 1st May 1821 the essays appeared in a beautiful edition of only sixteen copies under the imprint of S. & R. Bentley.

The volume, in large 8vo, was most impressive, as regards both the paper and the printed style. The book was adorned with a fine engraved picture of Francesco Petrarch, and in an appendix three of Petrarch's autographed letters from the collection of Lord Holland were reproduced. Each copy carried a personal dedication and the number of the copy, and in the Library of the British Museum is preserved the copy that Foscolo had destined for Thomas Greville (afterwards Lord Greville), the man who left his valuable library to the Museum.

It is probable that the translation of the text was carefully revised, and perhaps Maria Graham translated part of it, which, however, is not certain as Maria Graham was at that time seriously ill. But it is known that Foscolo sent her the proofs of the first two essays, particularly the proofs of the first, 'which is conceived so as to attract the attention of a lady, not only because it speaks of love, but because I have endeavoured to reveal the mysterious heart of the *civettissima*, and saintly Madonna Laura.' And the cultured Maria Graham, at that time thirty-three years old and married to her second husband, the painter Sir Augustus Calcott, wrote to Foscolo after reading the proofs: 'You say modestly that I can preserve the texts or burn them, but these texts are not for burning. What, as a woman, I love most in them is *the truth*. There are ideas that touch the heart and mind so much that as I read them I become involved, and imagine that in some former existence those passions and those sentiments were mine.'

It seems that Foscolo at that time had attempted English poetry so as to compose the verses addressed to Callirrhoe, which he put as a dedication to the copy reserved for Caroline Russell. One of his translators, J. H. Merivale, to whom Foscolo had shown them, had greatly praised them, correcting them patiently and lovingly more than once; and Foscolo, even before delivering the MS to the printer, had begged Merivale to revise yet again the verses that he had once more rewritten: '*Sans vous donner la peine de m'écrire, ayez seulement la bonté de rayer les variantes qui vous ne plairont pas, et de indiquer celles que vous approuvez en les plaçant dans le marge.*' It was with this final revision by Merivale that Foscolo printed the *Ode to Callirrhoe* in English as it appeared in the copy for Caroline Russell, which has unfortunately been lost.

In the meantime, the beautiful private edition of the essays published by the poet himself was received with great interest, partly because of its rarity, and the few copies were passed from hand to hand amongst admirers and friends. Lord Greville wrote thanking Foscolo on 24th May 1821: 'As a collector of books I cannot refrain from mentioning the beauty of your little volume and the rarity of the number of copies'; and the fashionable poet W. R. Spenser, who did not succeed in finding a copy, wrote direct to the author: '*Mon cher Génie, je suis reduit à vous supplier de vouloir bien me le prêter vous-même pour quelques heures,*' and was able to thank Foscolo on 9th June: '*Sans aucune exagération, mon cher Foscolo, votre Petrarque m'étonne et m'enchante*', and urged him to issue a public edition in the near future.

On 27th September Foscolo announced to Murray that he was ready to put in hand the edition for the general public. Lady Dacre had prepared the translation of the *Canzone all'Italia* and of the other, *Chiare fresche e dolci acque*, which however did not fully satisfy Foscolo, who admitted that although he found that the former was admirably translated, 'be so courteous, O Arethusa, as to give to *Chiare fresche e dolci acque* another thought, only one; and I beg this much of you because you are yourself an inspired nymph, and a source of poetry.' Lady Dacre agreed to retouch her MS; but in the meanwhile Foscolo had, strangely enough, met a woman who could recite splendidly and was also 'something of a poetess'. This lady read Lady Dacre's translation aloud, and Foscolo found it so beautiful that he sent it to Murray, and at the end of 1822 the essays were printed. In gratitude to Lady Dacre for her translation, advice and help, Foscolo dedicated the public edition to her, and composed the dedication in English, partly from some words written by Lamb and partly from others by Lady Dacre herself; but then, dissatisfied with it, he wrote another himself, which, owing to his mania for cutting out every unnecessary word, turned out to be too condensed, and at long last he sent Lady Dacre both dedications, asking her to decide which she thought more suitable for publication.

When the volume was ready, Murray delayed putting it on sale, until Foscolo learnt by chance that part of it had been used for an article for *Blackwood's Magazine*. He then urged Murray to put the edition on sale and it came out at the beginning of 1823. There are still three specimens in the British Museum, under the following title:

> FOSCOLO UGO—Essays on the love, the poetry and the character of Petrarch, comprising numerous translations by the author's friends, by Barberina Dacre, and others—London, 1823, 8vo

A book which tastefully investigated and analysed the heart of Madonna Laura and of Petrarch was bound to gain the ladies' sympathies, and Foscolo received many letters, including one from Matilda Hobhouse, daughter of an officer who died in the battle of

Waterloo, and niece of John Cam Hobhouse. She invited him to visit her and her sisters. Could it be that apart from reading the essays she was prompted to send the letter by the memory of a little flirtation with Foscolo?

The definitive edition, published by Murray in a handsome volume, presented the essays in four parts: 1. Petrarch's love; 2. Petrarch's poetry; 3. Petrarch's character; 4. Parallel between Dante and Petrarch; and in an appendix there followed: 1. Petrarch's Latin poetry; 2. Greek love poetry from Sappho to the poets of the Lower Empire; 3. Theory of platonic love according to Lorenzo de' Medici; 4. Comparative description of feminine beauty according to the platonic ideals of the principal Italian poets; 5. Unpublished letters of Petrarch;* 6. A Latin letter of Dante recently discovered; 7. Translations from Petrarch by Lady Barberina Dacre.

The three MS letters by Petrarch had been borrowed from Lord Holland's collection, according to a note in Lord Holland's hand in the catalogue of his Library: 'N.B. 1822—The three MS letters of Petrarch were lent to Signor Foscolo in the summer of 1821.' In that summer Lord Holland went to Paris, and when he returned the following year he asked Foscolo about the Petrarch autographs and Foscolo was obliged to answer that he was terribly sorry but he could not find them amongst his papers. He suspected that somebody might have stolen them and smuggled them to France to sell them; and out of courtesy to Lord Holland the publication of his own book which was all printed and ready was delayed, in order to insert a notice about the disappearance of the autographic letters. Everybody was concerned about the loss, but by a stroke of luck, after half Europe had been stirred up, the three letters were found in Foscolo's house in a quarto edition of the *Iliad*. And Lord Holland, the perfect collector, added a marginal note in his catalogue: 'Returned and deposited in the table drawer of my library, 1823.'

The disappearance of those autographic letters caused a great deal of talk. The claim that they were lost was considered by Abbot Meneghelli an invention to cover the non-existence of the letters, and he denounced Foscolo as an impostor not above involving Lord Holland in his deception. (Thirty years before Meneghelli had announced a work by himself on Petrarch, which never was published.) Many insults also came from the Abbot of Breme, to

---

* The first is dated and signed this way: *'En Valclusa Kal. Junii MCCCXXXV III Tui Studiosissimus Franc. Petrarca.'*

whom Lord Holland wrote a dignified reply on 16th September 1824, limiting himself to giving the history of the letters from the moment that they had come into his possession. Foscolo wanted to reply to each of the Abbot's arguments, and later produced his *Lettera Apologetica* which was a cry from a soul quivering under the weight of a thousand calumnies.

The *Essays on Petrarch* were the most original and brilliant work composed by Foscolo in England. The other works, and particularly the articles that he continued to write for the reviews, were slight, many of them published without his signature, and they often caused him shame, mangled as they were by the translators or the magazines' editors. Writing for periodicals was wearisome, due to the strain of finding topics of interest to the public, and having daily to fill pages and pages that had then to be condensed to three or four, as well as the fatigue of writing in French, as a language more suitable for the translators. It is surprising that Foscolo should have been utterly unable to write in English, which would have made things easier for him. John Florio had written in perfect English in the sixteenth and seventeenth centuries, as had Joseph Baretti in the eighteenth century, and in the nineteenth century Joseph Ruffini had composed his novels in English. It seems, therefore, strange that Foscolo should not have been able to master the English language so as to express himself with the style which he had for a literary language.

Besides his contributions to the two great contemporary reviews, the *Edinburgh Review* and the *Quarterly*, Foscolo wrote also for the *New Monthly Magazine*, edited by the poet Thomas Campbell. Between 1821 and 1822 he contributed articles on the lyric poetry of Tasso, Michelangelo, Federico and Pier delle Vigne, Guido Cavalcanti, Sordello, Christina of Sweden and Monaldeschi. Much literary curiosity was aroused by the article published in the *Quarterly* in July 1822 called the *Eolian Digamma*. 'Digamma' was a word that soon was to sound fatal to his ears. . . .

He attempted also to write tragedies, but inspiration failed him, and to console himself he reprinted the *Ricciarda*, that Murray had refused, thereby adding another debt to his printers. Now and then, to refresh his spirit, he took up again his translation of Homer, and sent the third book to Capponi, who published it in the Florence *Antologia* in which, in January and February 1821, there had appeared the translation of one of his essays on Petrarch under the title of *Petrarch and Laura*.

V

Meanwhile, Italian exiles were arriving in London. In 1818 Francesco Mami had arrived, forced to be an exile at the age of sixty-four by the deplorable conditions in his country. He had arrived with a letter from Cesare Montalti, written, unbelievably, in Latin: Foscolo at once helped him to find pupils for the Italian language, and Mami, who was very hard-working, expected very little and succeeded in a short time in providing for himself and even helping his more illustrious friend. The tangible result of Mami's gratitude was that Foscolo was able to write his essay on Pope Pius VI very rapidly, thanks to the material that Mami gave him. Mami was from Cesena, the birthplace of Pius VI, and during the years that he was in Rome he had easy access to the Vatican. Foscolo's essay, translated by Jeffrey, appeared in the *Edinburgh Review* in March 1819, and the discretion with which Foscolo had used his sources was highly praised.

In that same year, 1819, Foscolo also wrote the essay on Parga, the outcome of the visit of Dionisio Bulzo and the Ionian deputies in 1817 and the other deputies in successive years. In October 1818 Mauroianni, one of Parga's envoys, tried to persuade Foscolo to become their representative at the Commons; but Foscolo, who could not have been elected as he was not a British subject, declined the offer, accepting instead the material that Maurojanni sent him. The work of the Parga essay kept him busy for two years. The Treaty of Paris had placed the Ionian Islands under the protection of England, but the British High Commissioner, Sir Thomas Maitland, was an oppressive administrator; Foscolo persuaded his influential friends to help his fellow countrymen when they came to London to protest against the hard measures of the High Commissioner. In May 1819 Parga was ceded to the Turks, and one of their representatives, then in London, obtained Foscolo's help in presenting their petition to the King of England. Provided with new documentation by Count Capodistria and Confalonieri, Foscolo wrote an article on the question of Parga's cession, which was

63

published by Jeffrey, duly censored, in the October issue of the *Edinburgh Review*. This article launched a subscription in favour of the people of Parga under the chairmanship of the Duke of Bedford. Foscolo was intended to receive the donations, but the death of King George III in 1820 and the dissolution of Parliament caused many delays and much suffering to the Ionian delegation in London. Foscolo obtained a sum of money from Lord John Russell to help the Pargian delegation, and in thanking him Foscolo explained that the Ionian representative had accepted that help merely to reimburse him what he had advanced to them, and reminded Lord Russell of his promise to broach the question of Parga in the Commons, which Lord Russell did that June, but without definite results.

Nevertheless Foscolo wrote a short book on the history of Parga, well documented, and translated by J. H. Merivale, who was a warm admirer of his. But the book was never published because Foscolo, suddenly afraid of being expelled from England for his too strong criticism of the British administration of the Ionian Islands, and perhaps afraid also of compromising the friends who had supplied him with the material, delayed the publication of the book, and in the end suppressed it altogether.

During these years, to make a change from the bother of writing articles for magazines, and also because he felt that his inspiration was drying up, he turned again to his translation of Homer. It is certain that when Capponi left London to return to Europe, he brought with him the complete translation of the third book of the *Iliad*, planning to print it in the Florence *Antologia*; but for two solid years Foscolo kept revising it until the original, and better, form was lost.

The years from 1818 to 1821 had been very hard. Foscolo's health was not good: he suffered from insomnia, and spending many hours writing and studying was harming his eyesight. The love episode with Caroline Russell was by now dead and buried, and the years had gone by without any great work having been completed, except for the *Essays on Petrarch*.

Besides, the torment of debts was never ending. His cousin Dionisio Bulzo, who had so many times discounted his bills, now declined to advance any further money. Baron Trechi came to Foscolo's help, but we do not know how much he lent. To add to the burden of debts, he was seized by a passionate desire to defend his beloved Greece, and the news of the failure of the revolutionary movements in Piedmont, spreading quickly throughout all Italy, filled him with desolation. Forty-six of his friends had been arrested and imprisoned by the Austrians, among them Silvio Pellico, whose letters had always been filled with tender affection and brotherly counsels. Luigi Pellico, brother of Silvio, wrote from Turin describing the sufferings of Silvio in the Piombi prison in Venice. Quirina, on 9th May 1821, wrote of the disappearance of Count Porro of Milan, who had been Pellico's protector.

The shadow of terror in Italy in that tragic year of 1821 closed the first chapter of Foscolo's life in London. The second chapter was to start joyfully and full of hope to open up the view of a life such as he had always desired; but this second phase, too, was to end in disaster and flight.

Considered retrospectively, the first phase showed that Foscolo's character and nature were the cause of his unpopularity. London society was full of brilliant men who loved sparkling conversation and paradoxes. Foscolo, on the other hand, was not inclined by nature to frivolous and brilliant conversation and could not tolerate having unimportant questions addressed to him, or questions that he did not consider important, and was wont to reply: 'There are three things I find insufferable: the smoking of cigars, flies and people asking me stupid questions.' Yet he could, at times, captivate the affection and friendship of some, particularly the ladies. Love, however, immediately grew into a torment of passion, which often left him depressed and desiring vengeance. He was, alas, a mixture of extremes: his mercurial temperament kept him continuously suspended between melancholy and flights of impossible hope. He loved a luxurious life, but he was a most frugal eater, always extremely clean and proper in his dress. He disdained restrictions: 'I must go where I want to go, when and how I want.' Yet he could set to work like a slave to earn a few pence with his pen. Even in a big crowd he would lament his solitude, which was his way of indicating nostalgia for his homeland. His letter of March 1820 to Capponi who was returning to Florence illustrates this: 'I would regret not sending you another farewell before you see Italy again. I long for Italy so much that as soon as I have the means I shall transfer

to my poor home near Florence, if for nothing else than to be able
to speak Italian once more.' And to Caroline Russell he wrote, two
months later: '... *moi, ne pouvant, ne savant plus comment ni qui aimer
tranquillement et sagement, je suis obligé d'aimer souvent en fou ...*'

And yet the most extraordinary surprise of his life was waiting
round the corner.

The 'Digamma' Enterprise

I

The grand enterprise commenced at East Molesey; but its beginnings dated from many years before.

In 1804 Foscolo, then in active service with Bonaparte's army, was sent to the Italian Division which, on the Channel coast, was awaiting Napoleon's orders for the invasion of England. With his old rank of Captain, Foscolo was assigned to command the depot at Valenciennes, where English civilian prisoners had been collected from various parts of the Continent. Among those prisoners were Major Charles Emerytt, with his wife and one daughter.

Major Emerytt had been taken ashore from the English Fleet at Elba in 1800, at the time of the English occupation of the island. Believing that Elba, such a strategic and pleasant place, would remain English forever, Major Emerytt had asked his wife Sophie and his daughter Fanny to join him from London; and the two ladies had been delighted. But in 1802, after the Treaty of Amiens, the English had to evacuate the island. Major Emerytt, who had taken a liking to the local wine, conceived a personal hatred for Bonaparte and a fierce resentment against the English government that was abandoning an island so convenient for him. He resigned from the army, and as he was quite wealthy decided to remain for the time being in Tuscany. The family spent some time in Florence, where his daughter Fanny learned some Italian; then they moved to Pisa to be near the sea. But one day, during the summer of 1803, while the Emerytts were at Leghorn, the Tuscan police arrested them as suspected spies: a Napoleonic decree ordered that every English subject, man or woman, should be considered a prisoner of war. The Emerytts were sent first to Turin; but the Piedmontese, to get rid of them, sent them to Valenciennes in France—to the concentration camp intended for English prisoners.

The transfer to Valenciennes was very hard for the Emerytts. The treatment was not much different from that in an ordinary prison; the few prisoners were all kept in the citadel, the men in one big room, the women in another, and members of the same family could not meet except for meals. Sentries in rags followed them all the time with guns and bayonets; and others were stationed on the battlements. Women were further demoralized by the surveillance of villainous corporals. Major Emerytt, as the highest in rank of all the prisoners, presented himself to the commandant to ask that his ladies, at least, should be treated with the respect that even in war was due to the womenfolk of a superior officer. All he achieved was that some barracks within the citadel should be placed at the disposal of those families who could pay a rental.

In 1804 a new commandant arrived in Valenciennes. Captain Hughes must have been an officer of better class, for when Major Emerytt presented himself to him, he had the satisfaction of speaking as between gentleman.

Captain Hughes was not very tall, but well-built and elegant in the smart hazelnut coloured uniform. He had a lively manner, rapid gestures and a ringing voice. His head, however, was not that of a military man. One could not call him handsome, for his features were somewhat too definite, and his face was pale and lean under a vast forehead crowned by a crop of copper-red hair. But his sunken grey eyes, attentive and brilliant, seemed to suggest pensive severity, in contrast to his mouth, which was affable and sensuous.

Captain Hughes was most courteous to the Emerytts. Mrs Emerytt noted his aristocratic hands, and Fanny looked at him with kinder eyes when she heard that he was not French and did not hate England, although he owed one of his wounds to the English in Genoa. Captain Hughes had added that he did not feel hatred for any country, and felt contempt only for the enslaved peoples; and to Mrs Emerytt, who asked him if, with such sentiments, he was a cosmopolitan, Captain Hughes replied that a man without a country could only be a bastard; and he smiled sadly, a kind of romantic shadow on his face. He was Greek by birth, he said, a son of the Ionian Islands, from an island made dark by cypresses and shiny with silver olive trees under a hyacinth sky. In this loathsome fortress of Valenciennes, where he had been sent to perish, he considered himself at the service of his own country, Italy.

The prisoners at once obtained, from Captain Hughes, greater freedom within the prison, and permits to go round the town on parole until nightfall. The Emerytts were the first to obtain permission to rent an apartment in the town, and as Major Emerytt expressed his fear of not being able to enjoy such a magnificent concession because his funds were getting low, and he did not know how to obtain more money from his London banking account, Captain Hughes, who seemed competent in financial matters, offered to help through some Italian bankers who had dealings with a banking house in London, and who would accept a draft drawn upon London. Meantime Captain Hughes begged 'his English colleague' to accept an advance from him.

Thus the Emerytts were able to instal themselves immediately in decent quarters that Captain Hughes helped them to find not far from the church of Saint Wast. The day they took possession, the two ladies had the pleasant surprise of finding flowers in the rooms: Captain Hughes was, indeed, a perfect gentleman, and the Emerytts treated him as a true friend.

Captain Hughes was delighted to have some friends with whom he could spend his free hours. He spoke in French, with a few words of English, of war and peace, telling Sophie that she reminded him of his beloved mother who had been expecting him in Venice for many years. Now and then he spoke of his own life, a mysterious life full of misadventures and bitterness. With Fanny, who had been in Florence, he spoke of Tuscany for which he longed. Fanny found it pleasant to practise her Italian again with Captain Hughes, and she helped him with his English. He would have liked to translate some English work, and as he showed a liking for the humour of Sterne, they read *The Sentimental Journey* together. The cultured Captain Hughes, in return, read Petrarch to her, and under his training and with the help of his enthusiastic explanations, Fanny showed a striking aptitude for understanding Italian poetry.

One autumn day Fanny found Captain Hughes at the gate with a horse for her, and they had a long ride beyond the town. Fanny returned rather disturbed, but quite happy.

Towares the end of the winter, a sense of malaise crept into the Emerytt household. The family was feeling the strain of being prisoners. Fanny was growing nervous and depressed; Captain Hughes said his eyes were aching, perhaps from too much reading. Or maybe it was for all of them the fear of an impending attack on the English coast.

In March 1805 Captain Hughes suddenly arrived one day to take leave of the Emerytts. He had received orders to leave that very evening for Boulogne to join his division. He did not mention any possibility of meeting again, saying something about a dark destiny. Fanny looked at him with wide-open eyes, and the Emerytts were desolate.

Some days passed without anything happening. There was no sound of gunfire from the sea, nor were there any changes in Valenciennes. Captain Hughes's successor did not bother about the prisoners. Sophie was regretting the young officer whom she had reminded of his own mother. But Fanny was prostrate. To her anxious mother she said nothing. Two letters from Captain Hughes arrived from Lille; the one for Fanny remained unopened on the table until Fanny threw it into the fire without reading it.

With the passing of the months Mrs Emerytt noted a change in her daughter's appearance; her face became livid, and her body seemed to get bigger. One day her mother noticed that her daughter's ankles were swollen, but Fanny refused to have a doctor. Then her mother understood, and opened her arms. Fanny stood rigid, made desperate by her pregnancy. *His* name was never mentioned, but Sophie understood. Major Emerytt wanted to take steps: 'No,' cried Fanny, 'never! I never want to hear his name again!'

Nevertheless Sophie wrote to Hughes, whose answer made her weep. A modest layette was prepared for the expected baby, quite modest, for it was a difficult time for getting money from London. During the last few weeks of pregnancy Fanny became sweeter, and she and her mother chose a name for the infant. It was a girl, and she was christened Floriana.

During this period the French Fleet under Admiral Villeneuve was repulsed by the English Fleet. Major Emerytt announced solemnly to the family that within a month they would all be in England, and embraced his daughter with her own daughter beside her, the child of Captain Hughes.

II

During the few months that he had spent in 1817 at East Molesey as a country gentleman, Foscolo had been introduced by Miss Pamela Fitzgerald to a neighbour of hers, who lived in a pleasant little house called 'Emerytt Lodge'. Foscolo said nothing, but the name Emerytt had awakened a host of memories.

In Emerytt Lodge lived an old lady, with a young granddaughter of about twelve. The Lodge was old, with a fine small porch in front, supported by two pillars. There were no large reception rooms, but the house was still too big for the grandmother and her grandchild, who were living there with a cook who had been the child's nanny. There was also a stable boy who looked after the small garden. The little river Mole ran in front of the house, and the little girl was envious of the people sailing on the river in small boats. The grandmother was a gentle old lady, slender and pale, with silver hair under a white lace cap. Sometimes she told Floriana of the many journeys she had made in Italy with the child's mother and grandfather, who had been an officer; she told her of the delights of Elba and Florence, but she seemed to close up whenever Floriana asked her about France.

Little Floriana had lived for eleven years in London until her mother's death; and now she was happy to live with her grandmother at East Molesey. The vicar came every day to teach her English and arithmetic, and twice a week an elderly spinster came to give her piano lessons, which she liked very much. Her grandmother taught her French, which the old lady had learned perfectly during the sad years she had spent in France. During the summer, in the middle of August, Floriana had her twelfth birthday, and her grandmother took her upstairs into her own bedroom, and from a cabinet took a small chest out of which she took a locket suspended on a gold chain. When the old lady opened the locket Floriana recognized the miniature as being the young lady who had sometimes visited her in London. The grandmother placed the chain around Floriana's neck, and with her sweet voice told her things that to Floriana sounded mysterious. Her mother, her grandmother said, who had died young, had had two husbands and she, Floriana, was the child of her first marriage. 'When your mother remarried, she went to live far away, and she entrusted you to me, yet she always loved you'. Was there, Floriana asked, also a portrait of her father? The grandmother pressed her to her heart, and cried a little, and Floriana wept too: 'No, and you have never seen him because he had to leave before you were born on account of the war. Your father was a foreigner, fighting in a foreign army. One day I will tell you everything. Your father had to go away, and we never heard anything more from him. Perhaps he is not dead, and one day you will meet him. Do not tell anything of this to anyone.'

Time went by. The village of East Molesey became fashionable for holidays, and in June many rich families from London came to the cottages and modern villas; the young rode and sailed on the Mole and the Thames, flowing wide and majestic nearby; and in the villas the young people danced the waltz, which after the war had become the fashion.

Floriana made friends with the gentle Fitzgerald sisters: Pamela who was twenty and Sophia eighteen, who had lost their mother. Their father, whose business called him often to London, entrusted them to Mrs Emerytt.

One day her grandmother called her into the drawing-room, where she found an elegant young gentleman, whom she had already noticed because he lived in a cottage not far from the Fitzgeralds, who knew him. The young man was standing near her grandmother's armchair, bowing slightly and holding one of the old lady's hands. And when Floriana came forward he said, in a strong, warm voice with a foreign accent: 'Miss Floriana, would you like us to become friends?' And her grandmother added: 'This gentleman met me and your poor mother before you were born, when we were prisoners in France. In memory of your mother, it gives me great pleasure that he should meet you today.' The gentleman stroked her hair, remarking that it was almost the colour of his own but more golden, and then he asked: 'Will you permit me to call you simply Floriana?' And Floriana felt her heart flutter, and noticed that the gentleman's face was rather ugly, but that he had extraordinary eyes.

When she was alone with her grandmother, Floriana asked questions, and the answers did not explain anything. The gentleman, whose name was Hughes, had been a friend of Floriana's mother, but he had somehow misbehaved with them all. . . . Afterwards he met with misfortunes that gained him everybody's forgiveness and sympathy. In his own country, Italy, Hughes was famous as a poet; and now he was living in East Molesey, and he would come sometimes to visit her, perhaps often . . . And Floriana asked herself what misfortunes could have befallen Hughes, and why was Italy a land of misfortune, and why had he been obliged to leave it?

Was the meeting of Mrs Emerytt and 'Hughes' entirely by chance? Or was Destiny the hand that had led Foscolo to the old lady, who secretly had never shared the bitterness of her own daughter for the man who had abandoned her? Surely Foscolo would not have found it simple to present himself to the grandmother of this young daughter of his, whom he would have found difficult to present to the world, and about whom neither his mother nor even the kind woman in Florence, Quirina, knew anything at all.

Thus Floriana's old grandmother and Foscolo had come through a sweet path of sad memories to a merciful agreement, that both residing in East Molesey they would now and then meet and talk of their mutual friends and acquaintances from the time of Valenciennes. The education of Floriana would remain in the hands of the old lady, who considered Floriana as her natural heir.

Mrs Emerytt made 'Hughes', as she still called him, promise that he would avoid any word that might raise suspicions in the heart of young Floriana. Foscolo promised, and took care never to make trouble. It passed through his mind that perhaps one day he might, through Floriana, reach the shores of a safe and quiet life.

One day in the autumn, 'Hughes' came to Emerytt Lodge to take his leave: he had regretfully to return to London, goaded by his unfortunate affairs. Floriana cried, though she could not say why. 'Hughes' comforted her saying he would certainly come back to East Molesey in the spring.

III

One day, at the beginning of 1822, old Mrs Emerytt was found dead in her bed. After the funeral, for which an old friend and lawyer of the deceased came from London, Floriana was placed in a boarding-school for young ladies in East Molesey.

Two days later, at Emerytt Lodge, Mr Higgins read the Will in the presence of Floriana and 'Hughes'. All Mrs Emerytt's properties, the house in East Molesey and some Government Bonds, were left to her grand-daughter Floriana, and she entrusted her to her friends and lawyers, Higgins and Taylor, 'but especially, for the reasons of blood that Higgins and Taylor knew, to Signor Ugo Foscolo'.

To Floriana Taylor and Higgins explained that Ugo Foscolo, who at the time of the imprisonment in Valenciennes was an officer in the French army, had been compelled to leave her mother on the eve of their marriage, but she, Floriana, was his real daughter. In the interests of delicacy it would be better to keep the matter secret until Signor Foscolo could recognize her publicly. They asked Floriana whether she would, in time, welcome the idea of going to live with him and she answered that she would go most willingly. At this point Foscolo was called into the room, and he affectionately called her his daughter.

Floriana was now seventeen, and many times, in her imagination, the ties between her mother and 'Hughes' had been coloured by the romantic adventures of her age. Floriana was to remain at the boarding-school at East Molesey, the house having been sold, till 'Hughes' could send for her, as he was ill.

The first visit of the devoted daughter to her father's bedside took place in circumstances quite different from those Floriana had imagined. Foscolo was in a big bed, in a vast room, richly furnished, and full of flowers and people. An elegant lady was reading some poetry aloud, while the invalid frequently interrupted her. A young man was seated at a small table busy making a fair copy of an MS,

77

getting up now and then to ask questions of the man in bed. There was also an elderly gentleman, who spoke to Floriana very affectionately in English with a strong foreign accent, and Floriana was glad to be able to answer in quite good French. Then the visitors departed with great ceremony and many good wishes; and Floriana remained alone with 'Hughes' and the old gentleman. Foscolo stroked her hand, calling her 'my sweet young nurse', explaining that his illness was strange (Floriana learned then that everything concerning 'Hughes' was strange, oh so strange!)—a kind of bilious attack that could be treated only by taking black pills and sucking lemons; but what saddened him most was a sudden loss of sight, as a dark shadow with sickening flashes covered his eyes. Perhaps he would soon be cured, especially with Floriana at his side, and in a new house with a fine garden that he had in mind, with a piano that she would play. . . . Did she like the idea?

Then he introduced the old gentleman: a dear and good friend called Francesco Mami, an Italian exile like himself, and so wise, who would teach her Italian . . . Yes, Floriana was happy about this too.

Foscolo told Mami to find a book in the library, and looking tenderly at Floriana, he read in his lovely clear voice:

> *O giovinetta, che la dubbia via*
> *di vostra vita, pellegrina allegra,*
> *con piè non sospettoso imprimi ed orni . . .*

And Floriana, fascinated as if by a play, repeated '*Pellegrina allegra . . .*' And thus Destiny pushed her upon the saddest path of her young life, '*con piè non sospettoso*'.

To complete his cure Foscolo departed for the baths at Chatsworth, where he spent a few months, and Floriana returned to the boarding-school at East Molesey. Every week Mami visited her, and during her Italian lessons recounted the turbulent course of Foscolo's life, and praised his poems, and the example he had set to Italian patriots by taking the path of exile. He himself had, on Foscolo's example, left his native city of Faenza at the late age of sixty-four and had taken the road of exile, teaching the Italian language to earn his living first in France and now here in London; a poor life, but comforted by the feeling of freedom. For Foscolo, too, life had been hard; but now, Mami said, fortune had at long last come to him, together with Floriana's affection.

IV

The great plan for the house soon took shape. Already at the beginning of 1822 the two lawyers, Higgins and Taylor, convinced they were acting for the best, had approved the investment of the entire capital left by Mrs Emerytt, exactly £3000, in a plot of land that, according to a custom still followed in England, and particularly in London, was granted for a lease of 99 years. Upon this plot of land there were already two small houses, and a third one would be built according to the details of a plan that Foscolo was nursing in his mind. On 12th February a contract was signed between the housebuilder Charles Davis of 102 Great Titchfield Street in the Parish of St Mary-le-Bone, and Signor Ugo Foscolo of 16 Wigmore Street, to build a villa to be completed and ready for St Michael's day in the following September. The villa, to be built upon land belonging to Signor Ugo Foscolo, would have a lease of twenty-one years at an annual rent of £87.

It was clear from the contract that Foscolo had lost no time in getting hold of Floriana's inheritance, and in disposing of it in a hazardous way. Considering the tragic events that followed, it must be said that the lawyers' only excuse, apart from Foscolo's persuasiveness—he was a genius in the art of getting money—was the fact that the decade between 1820 and 1830 was one of phenomenal prosperity for England, and the face of London was changing rapidly, so houses and building land seemed the most profitable investment.

The situation of the land, upon which there were already two cottages and where his dream house was to be built, appeared to Foscolo enchanting. At the beginning of March he settled himself in the first of the two cottages, which was far from comfortable, and seemed, indeed, to have been built solely to let in all sorts of draughts, being all doors and windows—designed, as his friends jokingly remarked, to be fashionable rather than comfortable. But Foscolo replied that he was busy building a house according to his own

79

design, and in a letter to Lady Dacre, without mentioning the source of the money, and even less the existence of Floriana, Foscolo wrote lightheartedly: 'Being now reconciled to living and dying alone, my house will be no larger than necessary for a master who will never be rich enough to have too many servants or keep a stable. The rooms, however, will be large enough to contain all the books that will be needed by a man who is beginning to grow old, and foresees that his books will be his only friends, brothers and children, as they are his working tools. Age, and the misadventures that always accompany it, have prompted me to limit my house to one floor only so that I shall never have to climb stairs; and the garden will supply me with the necessary vegetables, and hide me from the neighbours' eyes . . .'

The letter not only showed his cheerfulness at that moment, but also that Foscolo was giving free rein to his most grandiose dreams. No more small houses in the country or miserly rooms in town! Now he was building a house, and building in a grand manner on a single floor, so that it would appear larger still. There was also an element of craftiness in that letter to Lady Dacre, in that he took good care not to be mistaken for a rich man by all the friends who had kindly helped him in the past with gifts and loans that he had no intention of repaying.

If he was not rich he certainly deserved to be. The famous 'Digamma' was merely a Mephistophelian vision: nothing, or very little, of what was in the house was paid for, and still belonged to the suppliers. The house was, so to speak, papered with promissory notes.

Engraved upon a handsome brass plate above the front door were the two words, 'Digamma Cottage', surmounted by the Digamma character (the now obsolete sixth letter of the Greek alphabet) that, strangely enough, was the first letter of the proprietor's name. It was the word Digamma that left people gaping; but Foscolo was so proud of his idea that he explained its origin to every visitor. Some little time before Foscolo had published a pamphlet *On the Eolian Digamma* which was, as the subtitle explained, 'an examination of the principal argument of the *Iliad*, to defend the poem, fame and actual existence of Homer, and to support Aristotle's criticism against the errors of some modern critics, etc.' That rather absurd dissertation had gained him greater fame among his English friends than all his other works and, proud and happy at such a victory, he called his new house 'Digamma'. He used also to say as a brilliant pun that Digamma was Greek for the English *Die Game*, a popular expression meaning that a cock died hard. Poor Foscolo! He too was a cock who fought hard to the end.

Finally, if not exactly on 29th September, as stipulated in the contract, but during the last quarter of 1822, Foscolo exultantly took possession of the house, 'prepared as a temple for his studies and a refuge for his old age'.

The sculptor Carlo Rossi, the cabinet-maker Stabbach, the decorators Weaver, Ames and Wilson, had all contrived to make the villa enchanting. Foscolo could now walk on Flemish carpets, rest upon sofas covered with zebra skins, sit upon rosewood chairs with morocco seats, work at a desk of African mahogany, and take his books from beautiful bookcases. In the drawing-room was a sofa with cushions of the softest down, round occasional tables of Amboina wood, two card-tables, fashionable chairs of grained wood with cane seats, three columns of imitation marble, one supporting a Medici Venus and upon the others large porcelain vases. On the floor was a vast flowered Brussels carpet adorned with small Persian rugs. In the library were seven bookcases of rosewood, a secretaire of grained wood, a round table for consulting books, a sofa, a large mahogany writing desk, chairs and armchairs upholstered in morocco leather, casts of Greek busts, three urns over the doors, and fine prints in gilt frames on the walls. The dining-room had a large round table of Amboina wood, mahogany chairs upholstered in green morocco, on the mantelpiece a fine clock, and another fine Brussels carpet on the floor. In the small study, the room for his special meditations, there was a huge copy of the Medici Apollo, and what we would call today a small bar. In his bedroom was a large French bed with seven chintz cushions to transform it, if need be, into a large divan; above it a canopy with damask hangings. The small bookcase was of rosewood, and there was a mahogany secretaire, a rosewood reading desk and bronze candlesticks upon the mantelpiece. Next to this room was a dressing-room with a vast mahogany wardrobe and a huge mirror. Thirteen rooms in all, all shimmering with colours and light, half for the master, the rest for the staff, among whom there were the Three Graces for the ebullient poet, in the person of three pretty young maids: Marianne, Lucia and Sophie, who caused Count Pecchio to say to Foscolo: 'The author of the *Sepolcri* instead of living with the Three Fates lives with the Three Graces.'

And the garden! No expense had been spared. In the small wood slender elms rustled among beech trees and cypresses, acacias and scarlet oaks, while lilacs and rhododendrons provided patches of vivid colour against a background of laurels. In the flowerbeds there were magnolias, camellias, tulips—a harmony of colours and scents. The Duke of Bedford had sent Foscolo many plants from Woburn Abbey and in turn, Foscolo gave flowers and plants to his noble lady-friends. Lady Aberdeen, in a letter of thanks, congratulated him on his success as a gardener, adding: 'The jasmine you sent me is most beautiful, and my room is full of its perfume.'

Yet another friend, Lady Dacre, wiser and less romantic, who knew how often he needed money, saw with alarm Foscolo squandering money on his garden, and admonished him gently, but Foscolo replied: 'The years, the troubles, the exile, but above all the solitude, have made me believe that in giving some thought to flowers I shall steal a few hours from the sorrowful meditation to which my nature is inclined, and the dreary work to which misfortune compels me. In the fragments of Alceo there are some lines in which the poet concedes the need for such pleasures to the suffering spirit saying that the more a brow is surrounded by grief, the more it must wear a crown of flowers . . .' Very fine, no doubt, but what a contrast with his circumstances!

The truth was that from the moment when Floriana's unexpected inheritance had fallen into his lap, he had behaved as if the modest sum of £3000 was an immense fortune. He wanted at any price to arouse envy, and to do so he scattered, as Scalvini recounted to Tommaseo, gold coins upon the furniture in his rooms, and suspended oranges and lemons with wire to the trees because they did not grow in England.

After the purchase of the land and the lease of the two little houses, there remained a decent sum for furnishing the house that was being built, but certainly not in the luxurious style that he had used for Digamma Cottage.

Foscolo had stupendous and ingenious ideas for making money and obtaining credit; but even by modest estimates £1500 had gone into the furniture, the garden had cost £200 in plants and flowers, and another £500 had evaporated in sundry expenses; and of this, next to nothing had actually been paid. At the beginning of 1823, that is after he had barely installed himself in his lovely residence, Foscolo was again compelled to look round for money, but he did not even succeed in borrowing from astute money-lenders, who declined to accept a second mortgage as security. Foscolo wrote to Lord Dacre on 14th January 1823, less than three months after having taken possession of Digamma, explaining that his potential lenders had declined because his deeds of possession might be declared null and void. He did not lose hope, and asked advice from his dear friend, the man of letters, J. H. Merivale, who on 16th January gave him the only practical counsel: 'I think that the only way in which you could raise money with your houses would be by an immediate sale.' Most practical advice, but how could Foscolo abandon his Digamma three months after having taken possession with such a flourish?

He tried to stave off his creditors by doing something less humiliating: letting the other two cottages that he had, by now, adorned with names in keeping with Digamma: Kappa Cottage and Green Cottage. And now began an involved story of miserable misadventures.

V

Towards the end of 1822 Foscolo was working at the preface of the *Essays on Petrarch* urged on by Lady Dacre, who had herself supplied splendid translations, indeed he never ceased to praise her translation of '*chiare, fresche e dolci acque*'. In the illusory serenity of his new paradise he had taken on as secretary to revise the English text a young writer, Samuel Carter Hall, and had installed him in Kappa Cottage. In the evenings Foscolo played chess with Hall, but unable to bear defeat, when he lost he tore his hair and threw the chessmen up in the air. Hall wrote some memoirs in his old age, and from *Retrospect of a Long Life, from 1815 to 1833* we learn that, with Foscolo, 'I had very little work to do, at least remunerative work, and at night I was very glad to retire to my cottage, from which the poet kept fetching me again with a thousand apologies.'

Yet, the young secretary found something else that deeply wounded him. This was the idea that Foscolo boasted, giving Hall the impression of living with an evil spirit. Luckily for him he soon got married, providing him with a good excuse to leave, as it was quite clear that they could not live together any longer. Foscolo's wickedness was too much for the virtuous Hall.

Kappa Cottage thus lost its tenant, and Hall was succeeded by John Banim, author of a poem and several dramas, including *Damon and Pythias*. Banim was a very worthy person, who in January 1823 begged Foscolo to let him the cottage, for which he offered, in addition to a small rent, his work as translator for one year, 'and every six months we will count the work I have done for you at so much a page, and if I owe you anything I will pay the difference at once.' But Foscolo did not like this proposal, and in February 1823 preferred to let the cottage to him for five years at a fixed rent of £65 a year payable quarterly.

But new circumstances arose which prevented even this remote possibility of making some cash. Foscolo had obtained from Kin-

85

naird the money-lender a loan of £140 upon the security of a generous but humble man of letters, Sheffield Grace. Grace had completed a work early in 1823 that would cost £200 to publish, and he could not meet this until Foscolo had paid back the £140 for which Grace stood security. He therefore wrote begging Foscolo to free him from the risk of being called at any moment to pay for him. On 14th March one of the Kinnairds told Foscolo that the matter was quite simple: it would be enough for Foscolo to pay Grace only £50 and to appoint a nominee and a lawyer who would meet Grace's representative, and together they would arrange for Foscolo to give Grace the £50. It was a very complicated transaction for such a small sum of money, but Foscolo accepted the advice, and on 26th March informed Banim that he had definitely settled the letting of the cottages with his trustees. But the trustees asked for a clear explanation of the lease granted to Banim, and having ascertained that part of the furniture was to be paid off monthly and part half-yearly, told Foscolo that he could not be considered a landlord according to English law. Banim was therefore obliged to give up Kappa Cottage as soon as the contract was signed.

But good relations with Banim had already been disturbed by the end of March through the eternal shortage of money. In January Foscolo had been able to discount two promissory notes guaranteed by Banim, using the money thus received to placate the furniture people; but when the two notes became due, one for £20 and the other for £25, they were not met. Banim covered them; but when he heard of things said about him by Foscolo, he was offended and asked Foscolo to apologise, otherwise he would bring an action for slander against him.

Foscolo, with his usual obstinacy, did not send the apology, and Banim went to law. At long last, in June, Foscolo sent a reply to Banim's lawyers, but it was not what they expected, since he actually asked Banim's solicitors to apply to his own. A bad business, and an ungrateful attitude towards a man who had backed his promissory notes.

At that time Digamma Cottage became the meeting-place for the Italian exiles who had followed Foscolo's example and taken shelter in England. For more than four years Foscolo had been supreme in London society and spiritually supreme in Italy as the great Italian patriot who had preferred exile to submission to the foreign tyrant. The revolution of 1820–21 had ended in dire disaster, inducing hundreds of the finest sons of Italy to choose exile, and the successive years saw many of them arriving in London via Switzerland, France or Spain, where their presence was considered embarrassing. England had become the Land of Freedom.

One of the first to arrive was General Guglielmo Pepe, who landed in England in the middle of August, escorted by Colonel Pisa and a servant. The name of General Pepe was already known, because the events in Naples had been of direct interest to England for years on account of Admiral Lord Nelson's long connection with the Kingdom of Naples. Moreover, General Pepe had personal connections with England, and Queen Caroline herself had expressed her desire that he should come to England. Pepe was received on his arrival by Marquis Antaldi of Pesaro, and succeeded in rapidly making a wide circle of friends and becoming a regular visitor to Holland House. His financial independence gave him a strong advantage over other exiles, who were, by dire necessity, reduced to finding employment as teachers of Italian.

After the feats of arms in 1821 in Piedmont and Milan, the exiles began to arrive: Count Arrivabene came in January 1822, with his old friend Giovita Scalvini, soon after the arrival of Count Confalonieri, Pallavicino and others; then later in the month Count Porro arrived. Many English gentlemen had travelled widely in Europe after the Napoleonic Wars and had met the better known Lombard patriots in Milan and Venice so that, when they arrived in London, they were received with open arms.

Of the various groups of exiles the most interesting was the one that rapidly formed around Foscolo. Foscolo placed at their disposal the two little cottages in his grounds on the South Bank. The first occupants of Green Cottage were Count Santorre di Santarosa and Count Luigi Porro, who lived there from April until September 1822. Porro, from one of the wealthiest families in Milan, had kept open house for all the foreigners of distinction who visited Milan, and in that way had formed friendships with many exalted English gentlemen. Silvio Pellico mentioned in his *Mie Prigioni* that he had met Lord Byron, Hobhouse and Lord Brougham in Count Porro's house. Count Porro was a brilliant and loquacious man, with what Count Arrivabene called 'youthful vivacity'.

In August 1823 another exile arrived in London from Milan: Count Giuseppe Pecchio, another of Foscolo's close friends. Before coming to London, Pecchio had gone to Portugal where he had met the Piedmontese exiles who were on the point of joining the Greeks. In London Count Pecchio was happy to meet Foscolo, 'who is the one I most admire'. It was Pecchio who left us a description of the cottage while the building of 'prodigious Digamma' was proceeding. The two cottages, and particularly Green Cottage, housed other exiles in the course of 1823: Giovita Scalvini, Count Pecchio and Baron Filippo Ugoni. When Santarosa lived there for a few months with Count Porro, each had a bedroom and a small study and between the two small studies a larger room as a common dining-room: 'and a quantity of comfortable armchairs and little tables, for Foscolo, to whom the cottage belongs, is a great lover of such furniture'. Santarosa and Porro remained in Green Cottage until the end of September, passing the evenings with Foscolo, talking of the hopes of their faraway country. One day Foscolo gave dinner to several friends, amongst them Count Pecchio and Ugoni, Campbell and Cyrus Reading, who left a description of that somewhat agitated meal. The conversation turned to orphanages and Foscolo, who warmly approved of their utility, said that the Protestant capitals of Europe gave an example of greater licentiousness than the Catholic ones. Santarosa, we gather, thought otherwise and Foscolo, being rebuked, got more and more excited, saying that in Geneva, for instance, there were far more prostitutes than in the whole of Paris.

'What is the population of Geneva?' asked Santarosa. Foscolo replied that he did not know.

'And how many are there in Paris?'

'Nine hundred thousand', Foscolo answered very irately.

'Very well,' said Santarosa, 'in Geneva there are twenty thousand; how is what you say possible?'

'It is true', shouted Foscolo. 'I read it in the *Almanach de Gotha*.'

'But if Paris has nearly one million inhabitants and Geneva only twenty thousand, it is absurd to discuss the question.'

'You do not believe me; I have but repeated the information of the *Almanach de Gotha*', cried Foscolo, and with flashing eyes he ran into the next room and threw himself upon the sofa in a fit of rage. Not until the following day was he composed enough to be reasonable.

*　　*　　*

Count Pecchio was housed in Green Cottage soon after his arrival in London. The future biographer of Foscolo stayed only two months, because he fell ill and was obliged to return to the city, and in October wrote to Foscolo: 'All is darkness and sadness around me. If you do not find a tenant for Green Cottage I shall be glad to pay you a rent of £1 per week, leaving you free to put up your secretary or anyone else dependent on you.' On 16th October they signed a contract for a whole quarter, at £2 per week, with Giovita Scalvini and Filippo Ugoni; but a week later Foscolo quarrelled with Ugoni. On the spur of the moment Santarosa took sides with Foscolo, but considering the friendship that bound him to both, wrote to Foscolo that same evening: 'Please read the enclosed. In it is expressed what my duty as a friend to both of you prompts me to say. You are too just not to approve my suggestion, and I am too truthful to abstain from communicating it to you.' The affair degenerated into the threat of a duel; and Foscolo, greatly piqued by what Santarosa had written, wrote back: 'I shall now have to conduct the affair according to the customs of this country.' And he had recourse to an Englishman, Colonel Jones, who, in a note dated the 28th, professed himself happy to be of service to Foscolo: 'As per your letter I will now present myself to Count Collegno as representative of Ugoni.'

The two seconds desired to settle the question amicably, and Count Collegno announced to Foscolo that the dispute was now 'happily and correctly settled and, I hope, to your own satisfaction.' Each party was to write a declaration that 'Monsieur Ugoni (for Monsieur Foscolo) through his friend Count Collegno (for Colonel Jones) admits his mistake in permitting himself unjustified expressions towards Monsieur Ugoni (for Foscolo) and expresses his regrets at what has happened.'

Ugoni continued to reside at Green Cottage until 16th April 1824, three months after Scalvini had left; but the fact that Foscolo preferred to address a letter to Scalvini asking him to advise Ugoni that within three weeks the lease would be ended, and a 'To Let' board put up under one of the windows, showed that relations between the two men had not returned to their former cordiality.

Another member of the group was Giovanni Berchet, who led a very simple and retired life, although his fine gifts as a linguist, as well as his commercial ability learned under his father, would have enabled him to settle comfortably in London; and in 1824, after publishing a little volume about the Parga refugees, he produced two novels, *Clarice* and *The Romeo of Mount Cenis*, inspired by patriotism, and these were followed in 1827 by *The Regret*, *Matilde*, *Giulia* and *The Troubadour*.

Count Pecchio, after his return from Greece, moved on to Manchester College at York, and in 1828 married Miss Philippa Brooksbank, afterwards settling at Brighton, the climate being more suitable to him, and there he composed various works including the *Life of Foscolo*, published in 1830. The best known of Pecchio's books was still *Semi-serious Observations of an Exile in England*, in which he looked at England through too rosy spectacles, but the best passage of the book was: 'The finest English sun is Freedom', which echoed the words of Baretti when he returned from the misadventures of his *Frusta Letteraria*: '*The Best Country in the World*'.

1823 saw the arrival of the Piedmontese Count Ferdinando dal Pozzo, former Minister for the Interior of King Carl Albert, but he led a most retired life, so much so that after eight years he was writing to the lawyer Pollani in Paris (7th March 1832): 'Eight years and more I have now lived in Britain, and I have met so few people that I cannot believe it myself.' And yet he desired to be appointed Sardinian Minister in London, as he wrote on 2nd September 1831 to Countess Caccia di Romentino in Turin.

Other exiles, Ravina, Count Palma, Bossi, are only names, and their number seems small, although in 1824 *The Times* published an appeal for a subscription 'to help not less than eighty-three Italian gentlemen, expelled from their land for having tried to improve the conditions of their country, and now in absolute poverty.' Nor did Baron Raffaele Poerio leave any trace of his exile in London, there being only a letter of introduction from Pecchio to Antonio Panizzi in 1832: 'I think that you may like to meet him. Besides it is essential that the Italians who are working for the *chimère qui se réalisera* should know one another.'

Mention must be made of Fortunato Prandi, without whom many of Foscolo's MSS would have been lost. Prandi who, like many others, was earning his living teaching Italian, met Henry Crabb Robinson and through him became a friend of Mary Wordsworth, daughter of the poet, and also taught Italian to Lucy Austin and her daughter Janet, and when years afterwards in 1840 Ales-

sandro Andryaie visited London after his many years of imprisonment in the Spielberg, Prandi offered him hospitality.

In the meantime Foscolo had resumed writing for the literary and
political periodicals which through the *Spectator*, founded by
Addison in 1711, gave England its lead in journalism in the discus-
sion of ideas and questions of politics and economy, and in the
direction of literary taste, as well as in its satire of prejudices and
customs. Those magazines sold anything from two thousand to ten
or fifteen thousand copies per issue, commanded a large and cultured
public, and used to pay their contributors between ten shillings and
a pound per page, and sometimes a special contributor was paid an
even larger fee. If Foscolo had known how to keep a balance between earning and spending he would have been able, with his
contributions to the reviews and his other commissions from the
publisher-booksellers, to lead a comfortable and decorous life.

Now and then, during those years, he took up his translation of
Homer because, he said, none of the many Italian translations was
fine enough: Salvini's was monstrously verbose, that of Cerruti too
colourless, and the splendid one by Monti he did not dare to decry
openly, but in circulation a quip was attributed to him: Under the
portrait of Cavalier Vincenzo Monti appeared one day the following
lines:

> *Questi è Monti poeta e cavaliero,*
> *Gran traduttor dei traduttor d'Omero.*

The truth was that Monti, when he had began his translation of
Homer, did not know Greek, and without the help of the many
Latin and French translations that he had received from Mustoxidi
and Lamberti and from Ennio Quirino Visconti—all eminent Greek
scholars—Monti would have been like Alexander Pope, who had no
such help in England, and produced an elegant but unfaithful
translation of the *Iliad*. And Foscolo, who knew Greek to perfection,
had a sixth sense for poetry, and he used to say that there is no poet
like Homer for capturing the harmony and the colour of words, and
that in no other poem in the world is there such passionate feeling
as in the *Iliad*. In his translation he preserved the energy of the Greek
text with great economy; indeed, he rendered the original Greek
text of 451 lines in 522 lines of translation, whilst Monti needed 609.
But although he had reached the Twelfth Canto, he only published

the First and the Third; and much to the regret and envy of Foscolo, Monti in very few years completed the translation of the entire *Iliad* which is still considered the best, whilst Foscolo in twenty years published only two Cantos.

VI

The few months of happiness that Digamma Cottage had given him passed only too quickly, and in January 1823 Foscolo had to come down from the clouds. The first shock came on the day for settling the tradesmen's accounts. Some were already knocking at his door, and the old system of incurring a fresh debt with Peter to pay Paul was less easy than it had been in the first years in London. His former reputation as a martyr of Italian freedom had by now worn thin, and he was now simply a man of letters who owned a splendid villa with all the elegance of a wealthy man. The illustrious friends who had helped him in the past did not even dream that he was penniless, nor could he now approach them hat in hand, particularly as he had not paid back what he already owed them.

There was nothing for it but to find himself work, and at first he thought of giving Italian lessons, as so many other exiles were doing and succeeding, however modestly, in providing for their needs. But the shame of lowering himself to do work which he considered too humble upset him, and on 14th January he confided in Lady Dacre, asking her to insert the following notice in all the gazettes: 'The author of the *Essays on Petrarch* is giving lessons in Italian, and will visit the houses of all potential pupils.'

'I feel, My Lady, deeply sorry for you and for all those who, like you, not imagining that I should end up as a teacher of languages, have opened their houses to me, believing that I should continue to live like a gentleman. But the enclosed note, that you will please give to your husband, will convince you that for the last three months I have been faced with the alternative of either putting an end to my life or taking the only course which, while it takes from me the title of gentleman, may give me the means of living like an honest man.' The enclosed note was the document in which his creditors threatened him with bankruptcy.

Good, kind Lady Dacre answered immediately: '*Pauvre Foscolo! Votre lettre me fait beaucoup de peine. Lord Dacre, qui a étudié la Loi dans sa jeunesse, aurait pu vous donner de meilleurs conseils: le génie ne vaut rien pour les affaires de ce bas monde. . . . Vous serez toujours Ugo Foscolo quand on vous trouverait labourant la terre, ou raccomodant vos souliers. Ne perdez pas courage, mais ne bâtissez plus de maisons.'* She realized the urgency of the matter and offered him all the immediate assistance that her sympathy and the vast experience of Lord Dacre could supply.

Whereupon Foscolo made a full and frank confession of his failure to find a second mortgage upon his house (which was not his own), and of the horrible expenses entered into with contracts that were now of no use. He said he had thought of committing suicide, but his sense of duty had kept him from taking his life while his debts remained unpaid. He had consulted his friend and lawyer John Herman Merivale, a specialist in matters of bankruptcy, and Merivale's advice had been to sell his house and cottages as the sole means of getting money, and he had tried to act on it, but the offers he had received had been discouraging.

Lady Dacre, who was a woman of sound common sense, came to his help with a beautiful plan: to give a series of lectures on Italian literature. By the end of February the plan was well advanced: Foscolo could count on receiving from his lectures about a thousand pounds, a sum that would relieve him of his financial worries. At the beginning of March the programme was passed to Lord Dacre, who made an agreement with the publisher John Murray to collect subscriptions for the series of lectures: the subscriptions would be handed to Lord Dacre, who would use the money received to settle Foscolo's most urgent debts. One hundred and forty people subscribed to the lectures, for which each subscriber paid five guineas in advance. This brought in £771, which suggests that some of the subscribers made the spontaneous gesture of paying more than the five guineas.

But alas, of this sum very little remained to Foscolo himself. At the end of the course of lectures, in keeping with his *folie de grandeur*, Foscolo gave a great dinner to all the members of the committee at Digamma, going to the extreme of laying a special road from the entrance of the garden to the front door!

Strange to say, Foscolo bitterly resented that course of lectures; he who in society loved to be the centre of interest, was feeling a morbid aversion to appearing before a crowd. In a letter to Lord

Dacre he wrote indeed that he was steeling his nerves 'to present myself to read in Italian to a public that would rather look at me than listen.' Yet the audience at each lecture was made up of his old friends, for the names of Lord John Russell, the Duke of Bedford, Lord and Lady Dacre, Lord Brougham, Thomas Grenville, Hudson Gurney the Liverpool banker, Hobhouse, the poet and banker Samuel Rogers and the Wilbrahams all appeared in the list of subscribers. One must say that it was most unfair on those noble and cultured patrons of him to write three years afterwards to his cousin Dionisio Bulzo: 'I would die of anguish if I had to taste again that most bitter chalice, to exhibit my face to a crowd of persons curious to see a famous animal, or offer him charity.' Surprising words which do no honour to him, because to give a course of lectures upon Italian literature should have been flattering for him, and as regards 'charity' he had only to reproach himself and his folly. Indeed, Lord John Russell, to whom Foscolo must have expressed the same sentiments, told him that to give public lectures in England was not degrading at all.

But although the £771 from the lectures had served to pacify his creditors, there remained another £871, and his creditors came knocking on his door again. The hardest case was that of the sculptor Carlo Rossi, who had good reason, as the previous year he had made a personal sacrifice to help Foscolo with a loan of £250, for Rossi had a large family.

Foscolo had given Rossi an act of attorney over all his goods, dated 25th August 1923 and Rossi, to make sure of his £250, had already drafted an inventory of the Digamma furniture. On 9th April 1823 Foscolo, before the series of lectures, had 'with tears in his heart', announced to the Liverpool banker Gurney that if he could not find a solution by the 20th he would have no alternative but to authorise Rossi to sell part of the furniture.

Rossi, however, better advised by lawyers, took 'technical' possession of all the villa before the appointed date, putting in his own representative, a kind of official bailiff. But as soon as this was known, the other creditors took fright, and called a meeting presided over by Rossi, at which it was decided that if within six weeks the creditors were not paid in full, they would immediately proceed to a general sale of land, houses and furniture.

The creditors, however, did not know that Foscolo was only technically proprietor of his goods, as being a foreigner he could not own property in England, and by virtue of that law he could invoke the benefit of the Insolvency Law, and leave his creditors with empty hands. In all fairness, it was Rossi himself who told Foscolo to invoke that law, believing that in this way his own credit would be better secured; but Foscolo disdainfully refused such advice: 'I would prefer to die, and much prefer a public sale of all my things, even if the result should not be enough to pay my creditors.' But the creditors, ignorant of Foscolo's propriety, grew alarmed and threatened proceedings, and for a start sent Foscolo, through their lawyers, a list of creditors, asking him to sell everything to the first bidder.

Foscolo, who always considered the intervention of lawyers as a way to cause delay, declined, and wrote movingly to his lawyer friends, Taylor and Roscoe, begging them to use their good offices to persuade his creditors to wait till the middle of June, as had been agreed at the time of the distribution of the £771 earned by the lectures. Foscolo hoped—and every hope became a certainty in Foscolo's mind—that in June he would have found plenty of subscriptions to the edition of the Classics, although it was still not down on paper, and upon which the publisher Murray had promised to advance a substantial sum. If fortune failed him, he would then be ready to return to the earth poor and naked as he was born.

His creditors did not relent. The most obdurate were Rossi who, poor fellow, was contemplating his own family falling on evil days, and Stabbach, creditor for £100, or more precisely 'the possessor of the Stabbach Bill', and a certain Lintest. Another creditor, Gregson, wrote to Foscolo saying that if he attempted to go out of the house he might be arrested in the street and taken to the debtors' prison until somebody put up bail for him. And this is what happened, because Lintest obtained an order of arrest, and three bailiffs went three times to knock at the door of Digamma. Foscolo had succeeded, during the night, in finding shelter with some friends, helped by the rule that arrests for debt could be made only between sunrise and sunset.

In any case, there was nothing else to be done but to pay Stabbach very urgently and also Rossi who already had his hands upon the furniture: it was therefore necessary to sell Digamma.

Ah, the sadness of losing, and so soon, the house of his dreams!

The temple of his studies, the haven of his wandering life! On 1st May Foscolo addressed himself to Roscoe, asking him to try to postpone the sale at least 'till the trees in the garden are taller', and suggested a way to satisfy Lintest who had become the personification of a nightmare to him.

But on 9th June 1824 Rossi intimated to Foscolo that he had given instructions to proceed with the sale of the furniture of Digamma. Some friends intervened, and the sale was postponed till the end of June; and, happily, Foscolo succeeded in satisfying Rossi, having obtained an advance on the edition of the Classics, not from John Murray, who had finally turned it down, but from another publisher, Pickering. At least the danger of the sale was once more averted.

And Floriana? When Foscolo had taken her to Digamma, three maids had curtsied in welcome to the young lady whom the master was escorting from one room to another. One of the Three Graces was assigned as Floriana's personal maid. Her room was simple and pleasant, and looked onto the garden where the weeping willows dipped their leaves in the brook that marked the confines of her father's property.

Life at Digamma had soon seemed to Floriana somewhat artificial —certainly not homely—and she saw her father only at meals, since the rest of his time was spent locked in his study. To the friends visiting her father she was introduced as Miss Emerytt, 'the orphan of some dear friends to whom Foscolo owed much gratitude'. Floriana accepted the fiction.

Soon, however, her father became agitated. For several weeks she did not see him at all. One of the maids disappeared, and the other two told her, in a rude manner, that they were not prepared to wait for their wages. Surprised that her rich father should keep the maids waiting for their money, Floriana mentioned it to Mami, by now her confidant, and Mami comforted her telling her it was just a temporary shortage of liquid cash. Fortunately, after the series of lectures, everything seemed solved, as Mami had forecast, and her father spoke to her quite cheerfully, calling her '*La mia Pellegrina Allegra*'. He also told her: 'This house is all yours, and one day you will share it with your bridegroom, and amidst the flowers your children will grow . . .' Beautiful words.

But suddenly everything took a dramatic turn. There were continual visits from the two lawyers, Higgins and Taylor. The staff was further reduced. One day, at the beginning of the winter, the lovely Brussels carpets disappeared from the salon and the library. In the small study there were, at times, violent discussions. The two cottages lost their tenants, and a 'To Let' board was put up. One day her father told her that if anybody called for him, she was to answer that she did not know where he was or when he would return. One night her father came home and began to weep frantically, and between sobs begged her pardon for all the evils that he had caused her. He spoke to her for the first time of debts and the cruelty of creditors. Floriana begged him to remain quiet for her sake, and helped him to find some books that he put under his arm before leaving the house, as only on Sundays the arrest for debt could not be effected.

This kind of life continued for several months. Floriana's only comfort was Mami, who insisted on sharing his meagre purse with her, saying that it was only a partial restitution for what Foscolo had given him, and adding that it was a great happiness for him to be able to live in London and give Italian lessons, while a man like Santarosa had had to go to Nottingham to earn his living, and Panizzi to Liverpool, and several other exiles were on the point of signing on as sailors on a ship that was going to Mexico.

Then everything seemed to be settled again. Floriana's father returned to Digamma, and resumed his work; there were no more servants, but Floriana was quite ready to do all the housework herself. The poet's plaster busts still made a fine show between the columns of the vestibule, and Digamma was, in theory, Floriana's property. . . .

In March 1824 Santorre di Santarosa called on Foscolo but Floriana met him and told him that Foscolo was ill and not at home. Yet she could not tell him where he was hiding, because on the previous day a warrant for his arrest had been issued on the insistence of his creditors.

Santarosa, who had called to say goodbye to Foscolo before leaving London, had no idea who the kind and charming young lady could be. But knowing only too well Foscolo's vagaries about women, he did not take much notice. Instead he wrote Foscolo a letter that is quite a revelation:

'I called at Digamma about 11.30. I went in, walked through the rooms, and I did not find you. The young lady told me that you were seriously ill. But where? She did not know. . . . If your abode is not too far away I should like to see you before my departure and embrace you; if circumstances make it possible for you to have some days of quiet, do come to me as to a sure friend. My poverty is only temporary, and I have three or four months assured. Do not let your troubles drag you down. Think of your mother, of our country, of the happy possibility of a better life. Do what your mother would approve, and let your thoughts of her be your anchor.'

Foscolo did not reply; he was oppressed by too much business and too many fears. Santarosa, who had news of him from friends, wrote again from Nottingham on 21st June, having heard that Foscolo was working on a new edition of the Classics, and was looking forward to a large profit: 'My dear Ugo, I beg of you, if you can manage to get out of your present worries and debts, do try to put your affairs in order so as not to start a new series of calamities. Great calamities exalt a man, while small worries only depress him and make him low.'

But the situation was desperate, and Foscolo could no longer choose between big and small calamities.

At that same time Byron, the poet, whom Foscolo had hoped to emulate in life, was on the point of dying for Greece and becoming immortal. And he, Foscolo, what was his position in so much folly?

VII

From the end of April Foscolo's life was one long desperate fight to get hold of money. His health had been deteriorating, made worse by the threat to his eyesight. His physical and mental condition was such that he could no longer face his problems. In April he had written to a member of the Greek administration, soliciting a job in Greece, but he could not obtain a passport. Setting aside his idea of going to Greece, he hoped to earn some money again by giving private Italian lessons, and wrote to his friend Stewart Rose who approved of the idea, but told him that there were other means of accumulating a little capital for his future needs. He reminded him of his own suggestion to prepare a new edition of Dante, and offered to help him.

Then Foscolo decided to develop his old plan of preparing an edition of the great Italian Classics and, encouraged by Rose, he prepared a programme for a series of nineteen volumes that would include Dante, Petrarch, Ariosto, Tasso and Boiardo. The first idea was to publish the volumes in quarto at his own expense, entrusting the printing to Nichols, but the subscriptions did not appear encouraging, and he therefore made an arrangement with the bookseller William Pickering of Chancery Lane.

At that time Foscolo was living secretly in a small apartment at number 1 Wells Street, near Jermyn Street which was, as he wrote to Lord Dacre, 'just furnished as the good God had provided for me'. He was still at that address on 21st June, as Pickering sent him a draft for £22 there for his work on an edition of Boccaccio.

Confined to the rooms in Wells Street by the fear of arrest, he had difficulty in obtaining paper and books from Digamma. The Classics edition appeared to be his only hope of success, and upon this he endeavoured to obtain a postponement of the sale of his house till the end of June. In the meantime the contract with Pickering was put on paper, and when it appeared that there was no longer any possibility of saving Digamma, Pickering advanced £250 to pay the principal creditor, Rossi, and disaster was avoided. Foscolo was able

101

to leave his hiding place, and he returned to Digamma.

But he was weary and ill. His sole comfort was the kindness of his old friends. In June, Roscoe sent him twenty pounds of coffee with a warm invitation to spend a few weeks with him; and a month later Lady Compton tried to persuade him to move for a few months to the Isle of Mull, where he could work in peace and economize. On 18th July this kind lady wrote to him again from Toroisk, off the coast of Scotland, to tell him that she had found two lovely rooms for him with a friendly family, and gave him all the details for the journey and of the very modest expenses: 'You will arrive here and stay with my mother, and you will rest and see the country; then you will go to Pennycross, a matter of seven hours, and I am charged to extend to you an invitation by Mr Maclean and his wife, to stay with them for a whole month . . .'

Foscolo acknowledged the invitations, but did not budge. It seemed that Digamma exercised a fatal attraction. The relief from his debts was very brief. There were no immediate prospects of return from the Classics; and the creditors started to clamour again, not to mention personal friends to whom he owed small sums. Unable to pay at the prescribed dates, he chose to stay put, but not all his friends were prepared to stay silent and many ceased to communicate with him.

In the autumn the catastrophe occurred. At the beginning of August Foscolo, always full of delusions, had written to Hobhouse: 'My affairs, that you have so kindly taken to heart, are now partially settled thanks to a remittance from my brother abroad, and it seems that Digamma, within a few months, will again be quite free.' Was he lying? And why mask the tragic situation?

At the very end of August he had further pressures and quarrels for £30 due to the brazier Benham. In November Benham was not yet paid, and his solicitors asked him to call on them to see whether it was possible to find a solution, but Foscolo was 'disdainful of dealing personally with a brazier', and spoke of 'using in my defence the law that he uses to prosecute me: I shall lose my small property, but my conscience will be clear'.

Benham sent in the bailiffs with a warrant for his arrest. Foscolo was thus arrested, but later managed to obtain his liberty on bail: and the editor of the *European Review*, Mr A. Walker, who in

August had accepted some contributions to the review, immediately sent him a draft for £54. Foscolo took it at once to Pickering to obtain the cash from him, but it was a Saturday evening, and Pickering could not lay his hands on the money without warning.

Another misfortune befell him. A small tailor, to whom Foscolo had given security for a poor Italian who had soon afterwards committed suicide, demanded the £12 that was due to him for a suit of clothes; and as Pickering had promised to pay both Benham and the tailor, Foscolo notified them to present themselves on the Monday to Pickering in Chancery Lane, but in the meantime Pickering had heard some doubtful things about the editor of the *European Review*, and sent Walker's draft back to Foscolo. On the Monday morning the tailor went to Pickering, and unable to obtain the money, he imagined that the letter he had received from Foscolo was a trick to gain time. In full fury the tailor obtained a warrant for his arrest, and the following day, 9th November, Foscolo was arrested and taken to the debtors' prison for a modest debt of £12 incurred on behalf of a poor Italian. This unhappy event took place at Digamma, under the eyes of the frightened Floriana, who ran in desperation through the rooms which were already almost empty of furniture.

That arrest was the end of everything. The creditors proceeded forthwith to the sale of the furniture of Digamma and Kappa Cottages, and shortly afterwards to the sale of the house and the two small cottages.

Foscolo was once more a beggar and an exile; and it was no comfort to have at his side the *'Pellegrina Allegra'*.

The Catafalque

I

All that followed was anguish and misery. It was his Calvary, and he seemed to foresee it himself. In a letter to Santarosa on 16th September 1824, one reads only desperation: 'For myself I do not see any other road that could guide me to an old age free not of poverty but of indigence . . . nor any redemption except death.'

The poet, who on his arrival in London had been greeted as a glory of Italian poetry and a paladin of freedom, and to whom editors and publishers had declared themselves honoured to publish his writings, was now reduced to working day and night to supply articles to magazines that did not always publish them, and paid him less than his due, and at times did not pay him anything at all. He became a literary beggar. Writing, a year later, to his friend and patron, the banker Hudson Gurney of Liverpool, he could say with all sincerity: 'Those who employed me made me work myself to death, and abandoned me to starvation.'

Once Digamma had gone he was no longer Ugo Foscolo, the author of *Jacopo Ortis* and the poet of the *Sepolcri* and of the *Grazie* and Homer's translator; he was no more the gentleman-poet. And his greatest tragedy was that he no longer wished to be. The Digamma gentleman had disappeared, and in his place there was a wandering beggar, humbled and miserable, reduced to fighting poverty and illness for the rest of his wretched life.

One comes to the conclusion that for a poetic and romantic nature like Foscolo's, the condition of a sorrowful person condemned to work like a galley-slave and to beg his piece of bread had a certain aesthetic value. He lived, indeed, the part of the character that emerges from his letters, and which could well provide material for a new epistolary romance. He disappeared entirely from the worldly life of which he had been so proud, broke all his friendships, reduced himself to living hidden away, under false names in humble districts.

To the Marquis Gino Capponi he wrote on 26th September 1826:

107

'I have dropped right out of society, and I live obscurely, trying to gain three advantages: one, not to waste time visiting and being visited; two, to hide my poverty so that the less it is seen the more tolerable it will become; three, and this is the most important, not to meet any more Italians who, whether as exiles or as Italians, are beset with discord and calumny; that is their fate which will follow them everywhere, and will be the sole inheritance of their children.' There was something melodramatic about those words, but there was also some truth, in that once back in their own country, the Italians who had been visiting him in London could speak nothing but evil of him; but the greater truth was that he wanted to hide his poverty. It is surprising that in such dire conditions he should not have decided to return to Florence, where the ever loyal and loving Quirina was waiting for him, and to whom he had ceased writing.

After 1823 his correspondence with the English gentlemen and ladies ended, and yet several of his noble friends were willing to help and tried to find him. The only friends with whom he remained in touch were the banker and writer Gurney of Liverpool, the lawyers Higgins and Taylor, Robert Roscoe and his attorney Stephen Garrad, who never ceased to lend him their assistance readily and with affection.

II

In May 1825 Foscolo left his little house in the village of Hendon, and transferred himself to Totteridge, a pleasant village in Hertfordshire. Now Foscolo was at long last free of debts, and could, in the healthy air of the country, contemplate some profitable work.

But would it ever have been possible for Foscolo to lead a modest life? In Totteridge he rented a ten-roomed cottage and furnished it with elegant furniture and beautiful carpets. Lovely sea-green curtains hung at the windows, with white muslin drapery and pelmets of ebony with gilt edges; a couch of red leather in the sitting-room, a lady's work-table in zebra-wood on a reeded pedestal with griffon feet, and some lovely Brussels and Kidderminster carpets in the sitting-room and adjoining room; and in his study there were red curtains at the windows, a roll-top writing desk such as had recently come into fashion, a grandfather clock in an inlaid mahogany case, and in his bedroom an ample French bed with hangings and covers of India cloth printed with scenes and flowers. In the stable there was a small carriage and the harness for a horse; and the kitchen was bright with porcelain dishes and china of Japanese make. All round the cottage there was a little garden, well planted and well kept. We know the details of this cottage at Totteridge because very soon it disappeared from the Foscolo scene but survived through the catalogue prepared for the sale. It did not have the exotic luxury of the fatal Digamma, but it was clear that Foscolo must have found a decent sum of money to furnish it.

But alas, his relations with the publisher Pickering and the editor of the *European Review* were far from assuring him a solution to his past difficulties.

His relations with Pickering dated back to 1824, when the Chancery Lane publisher had agreed to publish the grand edition of the Italian Classics conceived by Foscolo since his early years in London, and

109

repeatedly declined by John Murray for his failure to obtain a sufficient number of subscribers.

According to a first contract with Pickering dated 7th May 1824, Foscolo should have delivered every year no less than four and no more than six volumes receiving £54 on delivery of each volume. Each contracting party could withdraw, giving notice before the publication of each volume.

This arrangement was, in theory, guaranteeing Foscolo a minimum of £226 a year, or a little more than £4 per week, a very modest sum indeed to run a house and support himself and his daughter Floriana; but Foscolo, always inclined to optimism, hoped that this contract would set his mind at rest, assuring him the minimum necessary for at least two years, and left the future in the hands of God.

The reality, however, was quite different: it marked indeed the beginning of most bitter vicissitudes and suffering. The contract was signed in Pickering's house in the presence of only Pickering's lawyer; nor did Foscolo ever succeed in obtaining a copy signed by the publisher. He could not object, because already before signing the contract he had put himself in debt to Pickering for £250 that had served to quiet the sculptor Carlo Rossi and save the unlucky Digamma Cottage for a brief time. As for the £250, he had not been asked at the time to give any security, and it had merely been agreed that the debt should be reduced by deducting £27 on delivery of each volume—an arrangement that would have reduced by half the meagre income of the poet, but when the time came for the £250 to be paid over, Foscolo had to give two promissory notes as security, renewable until the full repayment of the loan, and give furthermore a guarantee in case of his death or stoppage of his work. And then the £250 had gone up another hundred for the purchase of books, among which Pickering had the cheek to charge even a copy of Foscolo's *Essays on Petrarch*. On top of all this there was the interest which was rising every month. When the furniture of Kappa Cottage and Digamma was sold, Foscolo handed Pickering £200 which was half what he had received from the sale. After which, reduced to hiding and saving himself from the creditors, Foscolo put everything in Pickering's hands, asking him to send him the books and what little furniture he had to Hampstead and then to Hendon: but Pickering claimed that those few pieces of furniture belonged to him as partial security for the remainder of his credit. Finally, in

February 1825, Pickering went to Foscolo with a friend of his, and compelled him to sign a note at four months for the balance of his credit: about £130.

There followed endless discussions, Foscolo contending that while his publisher Pickering was asking for such heavy guarantees to goad him to keep to the terms, he, Foscolo, had to be satisfied with vague assurances, and while he was forced to pay interest upon the money he had received as a loan, he could not claim any interest for the MS delivered, which was equal to the money advanced. Pickering recognised this as a just argument, but did nothing whatever to respect it. Altogether, Foscolo was totally at the mercy of his publisher, and now that his living depended entirely on the remittances from Pickering, Foscolo had to bow his head humbly, as his sufferings during the last few months had extinguished all his pride and will to resist.

Things went from bad to worse, because when in February and March 1825 the publisher sent Foscolo the first proofs of the *Discourse Upon the Text of the Divine Comedy of Dante* and Foscolo took his time to revise them, the publisher thought it better to use his own proof-readers, and charged the cost to the author, and as the publisher's proof-reader corrected the proofs only once, Foscolo had to read them three or four times. But this delayed the publication of the volume, hence further quarrels, till finally in July Pickering consented to pay Foscolo a fixed salary of £4 a week.

In the meantime Pickering grew alarmed at the news that another edition of Dante was on the point of being issued by John Murray, edited, it was said, by an Italian named Rossetti, a friend of the poet Coleridge. It was Gabriel Rossetti, father of Dante Gabriel, who had arrived in London the previous year. Pickering tried to push Foscolo to hurry, but Foscolo was not prepared to sacrifice the quality of his work; and Pickering, vastly alarmed at the risk of being surpassed by a competitor, suspended the miserly salary to Foscolo, and on 2nd August, claiming that he had not received sufficient MS for a page, he did not pay the weekly salary. For three days Foscolo was reduced to going round begging for money to feed himself and Floriana.

Moreover, the last part of the MS of the *Discourse on Dante* was delivered by Foscolo in November, a most unlucky month, because it marked the peak of the economic panic that had spread throughout England causing pressure on the banks and the ruin of many old financial houses. Seized himself by the panic, Pickering asked Foscolo for receipts for the money received, threatening to suspend any further payment altogether.

Nevertheless, the *Discourse upon the Text of the Divine Comedy of Dante* was published in November, but so full of misprints that Foscolo was in despair.

Thus ended 1825, and the new year started with signs of worse disputes and worse economic troubles for Foscolo.

Since the middle of November Foscolo had no longer received any salary from Pickering, and only in January was he able to pay his copyist, thanks to a gift of £50 from the Liverpool banker. Gurney was a true friend and protector and, according to Mrs Sarah Austin, 'Gurney lent, or better still gave Foscolo since they first met up to the time of his death no less than £2000.'

But if the last £50 came in useful to pay the copyist, it was not enough to pacify Foscolo's tradesmen as well. It was the misery of Digamma all over again: the tinker Buckland, the butcher White, the baker Coldwill, the candlemaker Bagget, and the milk-man, the coachman, the personal servant and all the others, plebeian and insolent, but nevertheless legitimate creditors who did not mean to supply or work any longer for this odd and somewhat mysterious foreigner. The daily battle with the various creditors became so rough that on 10th January Foscolo decided to take Floriana for a few days to the lawyer Higgins, who had chambers in King's Bench Walk. Higgins persuaded Foscolo to stay with him too, and the absence from the house at Totteridge made the creditors suspicious that 'Mr Merriatt' had taken flight, and one succeeded in tracing him to Higgins' address.

As the situation was beyond saving there was nothing for it but to sell the furniture of the house at Totteridge, and on 31st January Foscolo gave instructions to Robers' auction-room to arrange a sale, which took place on 3rd March. It produced only £102—not enough to pay his creditors in full. Not only that, but there was nothing left for Pickering, who was claiming repayment of the moneys due to him, although Foscolo contended that the debt should be gradually reduced with his work on the Classics. Pickering had Foscolo arrested.

Foscolo's latest detention in the debtors' prison was a short one;

but for him it was a descent into the darkest pit of the most humiliating degradation. Pickering refused any proposal suggested by Foscolo, and his own conditions were so offensive that the lawyers refused to consider them.

In the end, on 3rd January 1827 the lawyer Taylor succeeded in extracting Pickering's signature on a regular contract, but by then Foscolo was totally worn out both mentally and physically. Six contracts had been drafted by Taylor and all had been refused by Pickering, before reaching agreement with a seventh one. In the middle of March 1827 Foscolo handed over the text of his commentary on Dante's *Inferno*, but after all his work and trouble, the MS remained in a drawer of Pickering's desk till 1842 until at long last Giuseppe Mazzini induced the London publisher Rolandi to redeem the Foscolian MS for £400; by then Foscolo had been dead a great many years. Just as well because when the *Dante* was finally published with an anonymous comment by Mazzini on the two remaining parts, it did not have the success that Foscolo had hoped for.

III

The *Dante*, the first part of the Classics Edition, did indeed have many vicissitudes. As far back as 20th September 1818 Foscolo had announced to Quirina that he had secured a 'most advantageous contract' and that the publishers had been so generous because they were convinced that his works, thanks to his great and wealthy friends, would sell rapidly. Foscolo himself was convinced of this, and wrote urgent letters to Biagiolo in Paris asking him to send the Cominiana Edition of Paris, and the one of Zotta, and the *Biblioteca* by Fontanini so that he could consult them. But all he had written to his *Donna Gentile* was purely a dream, and a plan that was still in the air; so much so that in May 1817, that is one year and a half previously, he had written to Lord Guildford: 'You yourself, Milord, cautioned me from beginning the edition: what you wrote to me confirmed what the publisher John Murray had already told me.'

The real problem was, therefore, to find a publisher ready to undertake the cost of the edition of such a vast work; and it took a good many years. In the meantime Foscolo had published in the *Edinburgh Review* and other magazines his essays on Dante and lesser poets. In 1824 Lord John Russell, his old and faithful friend, asked him to supply an essay of some 50 or 60 pages upon the history of Italian literature from Boccaccio's death up to the death of Lorenzo the Magnificent, to be included in a vast history of modern Europe from the birth of the states after the end of the Roman Empire to the Peace of Paris in 1763 that had put an end to the Seven Years' War. Lord Russell's work was published in London in six volumes, under the form of *Letters by a Noble Gentleman to his Son*, reaching the death of the Tsar Alexander by 1825. Foscolo's work on this essay proceeded rather slowly, especially because of the upset at Digamma Cottage. It is not even clear whether the essay was actually completed and delivered. In any case, by the end of 1824 relations between Foscolo and Lord Russell were ended. The material in hand was used by Foscolo for various articles in the

115

European Review, and several of those dissertations, particularly the one devoted to Dante, were merely rewriting of the lectures that he had given in 1823.

On 17th April 1823 Foscolo wrote to Lord Dacre that he had accepted 'the advice of Stewart Rose who is convinced that an edition of Dante and the other Italian poets would be successful; and I have got out a prospectus, with some hopes that the idea could in future be of advantage to myself and to the English students of Italian Literature.'

The prospectus included Dante's *Comedy* in three volumes, Petrarch's verse in two, *Orlando Innamorato* by Boiardo in five, *Orlando Furioso* by Ariosto in six, *Gerusalemme Liberata* by Tasso in two, and Tasso's *Aminta* and lyrical poetry in a single volume.

It was his intention to prepare a definitive text, giving the variants of the more important editions, and to illustrate historically the lives of the poets, showing the influence of religion, customs and governments upon their aesthetic creations. A critical history with a psychological one, and Foscolo was the first among Italian critics to consider a work of art as a psychological phenomenon, and to find the themes in the souls of the writers and the ambiance of the century in which the poets lived.

When the idea foundered with John Murray, Foscolo found another publisher in Pickering; but, as we have seen it was yet another disastrous undertaking.

Pickering was a practical bookseller and printer, and he modified the prospectus, reducing the format and limiting each volume to 400 pages, though this sometimes meant publishing more, but smaller, volumes. But Foscolo saw the material impossibility of getting Dante's *Comedy* with the notes into four small volumes; indeed into three, because the first was to give the life of Dante with a glossary of the obscure allusions. To convince Pickering of this he delivered, in November 1824, nine or ten Cantos of the *Inferno*, by which it was clear that 400 pages barely sufficed to give the verbal criticism; it was therefore necessary to add another volume. Pickering, however, refused to pay a penny more than the stipulated price; and Foscolo, who wanted to denounce to Europe in general his personal enemies, offered Pickering the extra volume gratis, if the publisher would let him have 100 copies to which would be added as a preface a '*Lettera Apologetica*' intended to avenge his honour. Pickering accepted, and Foscolo put in hand the *Discourse on the Text of the Divine Comedy*.

But when in November 1825 the volume came out, it was full of errors and misprints. Foscolo quarrelled with Pickering, and no reconciliation was ever possible. Towards the end of 1826 Foscolo once again contemplated the publication of the *Dante* as a private edition, possibly in collaboration with Antonio Panizzi; but Foscolo's idea of prefacing the book with his letter did not meet with the approval of Panizzi who wrote to Foscolo on 4th January 1827: 'I believe that a man whose views may carry weight should be very careful in expressing them, should be generous in sacrificing some of his views to the good of the country especially when not to do so could have unfortunate results.'

Foscolo took this advice badly, and wrote to Panizzi on Christmas Day '*ad Apollinem meum referenda censeo*'. Panizzi did not expect such a rude answer, and on 4th January 1827 he wrote again: 'Seeing therefore that the country of which I am a son will be badly treated, I feel that I have not only the right but also a duty to reply. I believed that it would be better to sacrifice an opinion rather than inflame Italy. You think differently, and I will say no more.'

The friendship between Foscolo and Panizzi ended abruptly. It was impossible to reconcile the two men who, on the question of political history, were at opposite poles: two men who belonged to different times and generations, and could not understand each other. It was, historically, a sad episode; and the future proved that the calmer and more objective Antonio Panizzi had been right.

During those years Foscolo was also preparing a work on Greece, to explain 'the reasons for his long silence and speak in such a way as to be able to keep silent for ever after'. But the work with which he was most concerned was the *Dante*; and he had sent a copy of the stupendous *Discourse Upon the Text of the Divine Comedy* to Florence. Alas, the work received no more acclaim than it had in London because of the many printing errors. His revisions were a Herculean task; and anyhow, what could English readers understand from all that commentary which, in the translation of Foscolo's splendid Italian had lost all its impetus and beauty?

IV

The year 1826, after the sale of every stick of furniture in the little cottage at Totteridge, was a very hard year for Foscolo who was without any regular work or income. At the end of February, from two small rooms at number 6 Devereux Street, in the Temple, where he was living under the name of Emerytt, but was generally known as 'the German gentleman', Foscolo wrote to Mami:

> 'I am leaving the country for ever, alas, or at least this beautiful countryside, because my affairs compel me to stay here, and I cannot afford two houses. The young lady will come here to-morrow permanently; and if you will come next Wednesday or Thursday, you will find us here, but do not enquire for Mr Merriatt, but Mr Emerytt 'the German gentleman'. Do not ask about us elsewhere, for it is important that in this most gossipy place nobody should know where we are now. Therefore I shall transfer some cases of my books to your house, but tomorrow evening they will be transferred here, and the man who comes with his waggon will not be able to give our address. On this secrecy depends my safety, and on my books depend my work and means of existence. Without my old union with life, which since my youth has forced me to bear all the agencies of fortune, I should for some time now have been married to death.'

Three weeks later, perhaps for greater safety, and to cover his traces from Pickering, who from being his publisher had turned into the most terrible of his creditors, always with a warrant in his pocket, Foscolo moved to number 2 Duke Street in the Adelphi. So far none of these dwellings had been a 'garret', although Foscolo was often reduced to selling a few books to provide food for himself and the unhappy Floriana. What sentiments must have troubled the heart of the young girl, what painful memories of her comfortable life in her grandmother's quiet little house at East Molesey before fate had brought her and her father together?

In those months Foscolo had to sell the writing-desk and his

119

chair that the Totteridge creditors had allowed him to keep as 'tools of his trade'.

At the end of April he changed his address yet again, going outside London, and from there wrote to his secretary Giovanni Berra dismissing him since he could not pay him. He tried to write again for the reviews, and another exile, Fortunato Prandi, helped him to place them, for he had been in England for five years and had a number of influential friends. Two contributions, one on Boccaccio and another on Italian women, appeared in the *London Magazine* in the second half of 1826, and another in the *Retrospective Review* with the title *On the Antiquaries and Critics of the History of Italy*. This last was a vast essay, with eloquent praise of the works of Muratori and Tiraboschi. Foscolo must have done a surprising amount of research and documentation for the preparation of those two articles for which he was not at all well paid; and the poet was now merely a hack filling pages and pages at so much per printed page. The true story of those miserable months was told by Foscolo in a letter on 12th August to his good friend Hudson Gurney, thanking him for another gift of £50.

In fact, when Gurney's providential help arrived, Foscolo had really descended to the nadir of poverty. He had returned to London in July, and was reduced to seeking shelter near St Giles, at that time a most ill-famed district between the British Museum (then housed in a few buildings, before Panizzi developed it into the fabulous monument of culture that it is today) and the modern railway station of Euston. It was an ill-famed district, full of noise and filth, where the houses were squalid, and the streets at sunset filled with drunkards and prostitutes who, stretched out in a line, solicited clients. In summer the torrid sun beat through the dirty curtainless windows, and life was made more difficult by the lack of water in the district, compelling the inhabitants to go and draw water at the only pump, which was in Euston Square. In the letter to his friend Gurney, Foscolo did not mention this almost unbelievable hardship, nor was there any mention of Floriana, who must have suffered the indignity and labour of taking a pail to fetch water from the distant pump.

The good result of Gurney's gift of money was that it enabled Foscolo to leave that hateful place, and the same day he moved into a clean and airy little flat at number 19 Henrietta Street, where there was plenty of water, but poverty and suffering had increased his liver pains, and the sleepiness which was a symptom of the disease made it more difficult to work. Ideas for magazine articles passed through his mind, and for a kind of novel, and for the completion of his edition of Dante, but the dispute with Pickering still continued. In his letter to Gurney Foscolo mentioned that the novel was almost finished and already in the hands of a translator; but there is no trace of it, and it still seems incredible that after ten years in London Foscolo could not write in English, thus simplifying his work and increasing his production.

He planned a series of three novels, under the rather strange title of *My First Voyage to England, My Second Voyage to England, My Third Voyage to England*. Did he have in mind some light and amusing little volume in the manner of the *Sentimental Journey* that, many years before, he had translated in Milan and published under the nom-de-plume of Didimo Chierico? We know only that the first two would have described English high society and middle class, and the last one the lower classes. It seems that the second volume was ready; and from his letters to Lady Dacre we learn that this second volume would tell the story of his love for 'Callirrhoe'. From the publication of those novels, surely existing only in his mind, Foscolo was looking forward to realizing a sum sufficient to provide for many years, but it was only a dream.

During those months he planned also to publish the first volume of his translation of the *Iliad*, with a comment similar to that in the Dante, and a *Letter to the Greek People*. This kept him busy for some time, and he wrote about it to Nicola Piccolo, a man of letters and professor of Greek, asking him about the condition of literature in Greece. And he also thought of returning to his native isles: it seemed that his native Zante might have granted him modest employment and perhaps tranquillity to write some of the works that were gathering in his fertile mind.

He also had a strange impulse, certainly dictated by the remorse at the misery he had caused Floriana and the desire to make amends, and he took advantage of the departure of a messenger who was travelling to Greece to send the full story of his unhappy life in London. His confession was written to three people: his cousin Dionisio Bulzo, the Marquis Gino Capponi and his sister Rubina. All those letters were written during the last week of September 1826. To the messenger, a certain Reinaud, he gave instructions to find him a house in the Greek countryside, with a garden of fruit trees and a vine trellis. Not even his changing fortunes had killed in him the mania of younger years, to ask a friend to find him a lovely house with orchard and garden! To his cousin Bulzo he expressed his dreams for the future: he was not attracted by public life in a Greece that was under foreign domination, and preferred to choose the aim of guiding his fellow citizens to philosophy and letters. The lessons that he would hold in the Academy of Zante would exalt his mind and not humiliate him like the lectures he had given in London in 1823. As proof of his Ionic citizenship he repeated to Bulzo his determination to produce his genealogy according to the documents in the Venetian archives. There was also a letter written by his brother Giulio on 1st April 1826 from Grotz Blasnitz in Moravia and sent to London through a friend named Monticelli, and this letter supported Foscolo's promise, for his brother Giulio's letter enclosed a drawing of the family crest.

During the last few months of 1826 he composed two articles, *The History of the Democratic Constitution of Venice*, suggested to him by the Memoirs of Casanova, and the *Venetian Memoirs of Giovanni Galliccioli*, which had been published in London in 1826. Prandi had introduced Foscolo to Mrs Sarah Austin, who offered to translate the two articles into English. Sarah Austin's house was at that time a literary centre, but Foscolo took offence at her delay in preparing the translations, and then did not find them satisfactory. Many letters were exchanged, from which it is obvious that Foscolo's attitude caused Mrs Austin to dislike him as, many years afterwards, she admitted to Sainte-Hilaire. Foscolo withdrew the article on the constitution of Venice, which was later translated by Thomas Roscoe, and after being refused by Murray was at long last published in the *Westminster Review* in January 1827, Foscolo's payment being £40. The other article, translated by Sarah Austin, was accepted by Jeffrey for the *Edinburgh Review*. Incidentally, the lady's antagonism was caused by the strange life Foscolo was leading at the time of the Digamma fiasco.

V

Towards the end of the year his health deteriorated so much that he decided not to write any more articles and to carry on simply giving Italian lessons. He chose to go back and live in the country. keeping a room in town where he could meet his pupils. He found lodgings in Turnham Green, not far from Holland House which had been the scene of his first successes in the high society of London which had by now totally forgotten him.

Notwithstanding his efforts, the work on Dante was not progressing as fast as Pickering expected. The publisher did not believe that to write a reasoned discourse it was necessary to read so many books and meditate over them, and every day he called on Foscolo trying to goad him on. Foscolo had escaped from the hands of his creditors merely to fall into the hands of an individual no less hard to whom he now owed even his thoughts and ideas. The final agreement with Pickering had been signed on 3rd January 1827 and, according to the terms, Foscolo was to deliver by 15th March the MS of the remaining volumes on Dante; on delivery Pickering would have paid to Foscolo £167 and returned to him all the promissory notes he held; then Pickering would hand Foscolo one hundred copies of the first volume already printed, and, when the edition was completed, the copyright would belong to Pickering.

At the end of April Foscolo was installed in Bohemia House at Turnham Green, so called because, according to tradition, the Queen of Bohemia had once stayed there. The house was modest but comfortable, and the country around it was healthy and open. Not far from it rose the Palladian villa of the Duke of Devonshire, a classical residence surrounded by a vast park. Only a few friends knew Foscolo's address, but those who came to visit him at Bohemia House remained loyal to the end. Prandi tried for some time to place Foscolo's magazine articles; Doctor Negri, an exile from Parma, assisted him professionally during his long illness; Francesco Mami, his real confidant, often kept him company; Canon Riego, a Spanish exile, sent through Mami gifts of good food and often visited him personally; Giulio Bossi rendered many services and Foscolo reciprocated with contributions to his *Anthology of Italian Poets*. No less affectionate were his English friends: the two lawyers who had helped to settled his troubled affairs; Sinclair Cullen, Edgar Taylor and Robert Roscoe; the banker Hudson Gurney from Liverpool regularly sent gifts of money; and Charles Fox, illegitimate son of Lord Holland, and Lord Holland himself who, as soon as he heard of Foscolo's illness, sent him regular presents of bottles of fine wines. The poet found great comfort in the realization that his great and noble friends had not forgotten him. His illness and miserable situation had not extinguished his pride and courage, as is evident from a letter written to Canon Riego on 3rd August: 'Gratitude gives me strength to take up my pen and thank you for your letter and your gifts. But I beg you not to send me anything more, and let it be one of my last prayers, that you should not address any living person, man or woman, to tell them of my situation and obtain some help. I say this because I have heard something from Floriana and your kindness would only wound me further. Adieu. We shall be waiting for you tomorrow, if you are able to come. Adieu again with all my heart.'

His devotion to Floriana was increasing the sympathy and devotion of all his friends, and Foscolo kept repeating the sweet lie that 'the old wedding' imposed on him the task of living to provide for his natural daughter, and the years of poverty that had followed the sale of Digamma were 'a kind of atonement for my past improvidence'. This idea of atonement was now fixed in his mind, and already in December 1826, writing to his friend Jonathan Hatfield of Manchester, he said: 'I am reduced to living like a refugee placed outside society; but I have the satisfaction of having with these three years of labour, of privations and tenacity, atoned for my errors.'

Until June he was fit to go to town for the lessons to his few pupils. In April, prompted by Colonel Jones, the banker Gurney and Francis Cohen (better known under the maternal name of Palgrave), he sent his application for the Chair of Italian Letters at the new University of London. Later on he heard that the Chair would have been nothing more than teaching the Italian language, and withdrew his application. (The Chair went to Antonio Panizzi, who indeed found the appointment a great disappointment.) At that point the dropsy from which Foscolo was suffering became more acute. At the beginning of the summer he underwent an operation, but did not feel much better, for the dropsy returned very rapidly, and he intimated to his friends that he felt death very near. At the end of August Gurney, informed by friends of Foscolo's serious condition, came to London to visit him, and found him unable to speak. Suddenly, with an enormous effort, the dying poet launched on a flood of eloquence.

On 4th September the doctors carried out a second operation, but the invalid was so weak that he did not recover strength. With a final desperate effort he wrote in capital letters a moving message for his daughter Floriana. This was at the same time his admission of paternity and his last Will:

'DEAR DAUGHTER—THE MONEY HAS BEEN PAID— LEAVE FIFTY POUNDS TO OUR FRIEND, MR ROBERTS, TO ENABLE HIM TO REIMBURSE HIMSELF AND PAY SOME SMALL BILLS—AND KEEP THE REST FOR YOUR- SELF—YOUR FATHER.'

On the same day the solicitor Taylor wrote again to Mr Gurney in Liverpool: 'I went last night to visit our friend Foscolo and found him near the end. Doctor Lawrence very kindly visits him. Today they will again draw off his water.'

This paracenteses or draining weakened him very much. The doctors had already done it twice, and the second time, due to the enormous quantity of fluid taken away, he remained so weak that he worsened rapidly, and on the 7th, after the last tapping, he lost his power of speech, and ceased to recognize anyone. A few days before he had said to Giulio Bossi (who reported it to Panizzi) that Floriana certainly was his daughter, and he had given Bossi a brief summary of the whole story. Taylor, in a letter to Gurney, said: 'If Foscolo goes on for a long time I fear he will kill his daughter. The poor man gives her no peace, and the child is terribly pale. And if she were to die I do not see who could look after him in his last days. . . .'

Taylor had to go away from London, and before leaving he gave Roscoe the money that Foscolo had handed to him, the last £50 sent by Gurney, and asked him to inform Gurney of Foscolo's serious condition. On 8th September Roscoe duly wrote to Gurney: 'I have just now come back from Turnham Green. F. was in a sort of coma, and apparently not in much pain; but he is in such a state that it is almost impossible to get any sense out of him. While I was with him he opened his eyes, and said 'I love you', and when I asked how he was feeling, he murmured 'I am dying'. This was all he said. Perhaps he will go on another few days, but I think he is at the end.'

From the 7th he had lost his power of speech almost completely, and did not recognize anyone. The following day Count Capodistria, who had arrived the previous day, was shocked to find Foscolo in such a state and be unable to converse with him.

Taylor had already communicated to Gurney that he was uncertain 'what we could do for his funeral and settling his few things, as well as scraping up as much as possible for the poor girl, whose self-denial deserves the highest praise.' Floriana had told him that Foscolo had expressed a desire to be buried quietly in Chiswick cemetery, and had told Taylor the same. 'Yet,' Taylor wrote, 'there is not much, because Foscolo has nothing but a few books and some bits of furniture and the money that is in my hands, and that must be used for immediate needs.'

He died on 10th September. Roscoe informed Gurney at once: 'You will be grieved but not surprised to read that the object of your constant friendship and kindness, poor Foscolo, has drawn his last breath. He died last evening, about 8.30. Doctor Negri said that he could not have suffered much. . . . He is to be buried in Chiswick cemetery, and the funeral will take place on Monday or Tuesday next. I have arranged for a decent funeral though quite modest.'

His five faithful friends buried him in the cemetery of the Parish of Chiswick: Canon Riego, Doctor Negri, Francesco Mami, General De Meistre and the historian Edward Roscoe, and on 29th September the *Literary Chronicle* and *Weekly Review* published a letter signed by several admirers: 'While Europe is admiring the works of the exile, his grave shows that there were, in this country, people who admired his talents, while deploring the errors of his life. Such errors have ceased to exist, and it is to his genius alone that we propose to offer a small token of respect.'

Donations were to be sent to Pickering, the publisher, but apparently the idea did not produce very much.

Later on Gurney had a stone slab put on the grave, giving the date of the poet's death and his age; but both dates were wrong. Later still Gurney replaced the stone, worn by the feet of the people visiting the cemetery, and erected a small tomb in the shape of an altar.

Floriana disappeared. From Florence Quirina, loyal and generous as ever, tried to trace her, but only heard that after some help from Mami, she had moved to Manchester as a teacher of languages. Then, after a brief period of happiness Floriana died of consumption at the age of twenty-two. A sad end for the '*Pellegrina Allegra*'. Quirina could do no more than to beg all Foscolo's friends to collect the papers of her poet.

Today, in Chiswick cemetery above the old grave stands a great tomb of marble that records the removal of his mortal remains to the Temple of Santa Croce in Florence, and a wreath of laurel encloses his line: '*Giusta di glorie dispensiera è Morte*'. And still today the little cemetery next to the old church is like the cemetery of which Foscolo had sung, and his memory is preserved '*all'ombra dei cipressi*'.